medical
school

SURVIVAL GUIDE

D0495649

WITHDRAWN

trauma

for medical students ... by medical students

trauma

First edition 2004

trauma Publishing
PO Box 36434
London
EC1M 6WA

T 0207 3620488
F 0870 1306985

books@traumaroom.com
http://www.traumaroom.com

ISBN 0-9547657-0-2

Printed in the UK by Witherbys, London

medical
school

SURVIVAL
GUIDE

about
this book

starting out

arriving at medical school on that ominous first day is enough to fill even the bravest student with a deep sense of dread. It's a scary experience, and so it should be. While your friends are off learning to cross-stitch you'll be spending time with your hands deep in someone's chest.

This book is designed not just to get you through the first few weeks or the first year, it will hopefully help you at all stages of your medical school career from a confused fresher right up to a newly qualified junior doctor.

It is the 'Book of Life' of over a hundred students who have gone through the highs and lows of a six year medical education. This is how they coped. From those who got distinctions and prizes, to those who dropped (or were kicked) out. It's all here, the good and the bad.

Over the next six years you will experience some of the best and worst moments of your life. Just remember that thousands of medical students have gone before you and survived. We hope that this book will help you experience more of the highs and a little less of the lows.

Medical school is a great experience. You've been lucky enough to be given a place. Do your best to enjoy both the good and the bad and we can promise that you'll never regret it. Good luck and may we wish you a safe and successful journey.

The *trauma* Team

medical school　SURVIVAL GUIDE

over 55,000

medical students ...

more than

22 countries

trauma

welcome to the world's <u>largest</u>
free distribution student magazine

about trauma

*t**rauma** is the magazine for medical students—produced by medical students. Formed by students four years ago it is distributed free in all UK medical schools four times each year. Our international edition is available in 22 countries worldwide from Belize to Zambia—making us the world's largest free distribution student magazine!!*

All our stories are written by students about topics they want to read. The latest news, features and resources have helped make *trauma* one of the top sources for information among the medical community. Freshers, elective and careers supplements support the content of our main magazine. We also compile the UK's only list of 180 intercalated courses which are becoming an increasingly important part of the medical degree course.

Our unique rep structure means that we have a presence in each medical school across the UK and around the world. The '*trauma* Team' of over 100 people help ensure copies reach students through the medical schools, libraries and student unions. We keep our team informed of the latest updates through our '*trauma* Team Talk' email list.

Online we offer students the web version of *trauma* along with access to the '*trauma* Community'. Free student email accounts, discussion boards and scheduled chat help bring our readers from around the world together. We also help students publish their work online and offer revision resources.

Produced entirely by medical students in their free-time we're extremely proud of our achievements over the past four years. Our presence in all corners of the globe is proof of the enthusiasm, energy and fun of the '*trauma* team' and '*trauma*' magazine.

Check us out and get involved at ***www.traumaroom.com***

medical school   SURVIVAL GUIDE

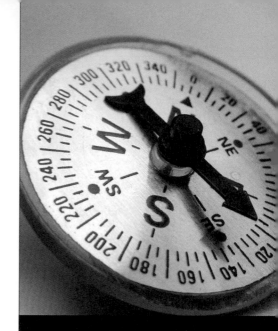

medical
school

SURVIVAL
GUIDE

becoming
a doctor

starting out

medical school can be a scary place. There's the dissection room, angry hospital consultants and the student union bar on a Wednesday night. But don't go running for home just yet.

With the help of medical students who have been there and survived with most of their limbs intact, we'll tell you how to survive in the land of colonoscopy clinics, cardiac vivas and neuro MCQs.

So put on that white coat, swing that stethoscope round your neck and step out into the big bad world of becoming a doctor. We start with the essential induction to your new life.

trust me i'm (almost) a doctor

Ask most patients what a 'medical student' is and they'll screw up their eyes in confusion. Patients see you trailing around after the real doctors in your smart white coat and often view you in the same medically qualified club. As such you've unwittingly become a privileged member of society's most trusted profession.

As a medical student you'll spend more time with patients than any other person in the team. You're in that middle-ground between being a member of the public and a medical professional. Patients won't find you quite as scary as a proper doctor and you'll be making an extra special effort to suck up in order to take their medical history.

Because of this they'll tell you things they've never told anyone and you'll witness grown men break down in tears behind that thin, flimsy cubicle curtain. It's all part of becoming a doctor – and a good one at that.

Just don't abuse it. Patients trust you with this information and you're legally bound to confidentiality. So no blabbing about it down the pub, it could be the patient's relatives

SURVIVAL GUIDE   *medical school*

at the next table. Medical students have been kicked out of medical school on a number of occasions for abusing this – and they've no defence.

Unlike those other students studying embroidery or pole dancing, you're going to have to do some hard studying during the course. You've made it to medical school which proves you've got a few brain cells – but don't let this go to that straight-'A' head of yours.

Medicine is one of those subjects which trumps the 'A-levels are the hardest exams you'll ever do' line – in fact, it rips this theory to shreds, throws it on the ground and stomps all over it. Medicine is tough and there's no escaping that.

But don't get disheartened if you only scraped into medical school by the skin of your teeth and the number of zeros on daddy's cheque to the alumni association, you don't need to be a whizzkid to pick up a MBBS. A little common sense and good organisation is all you need. Medicine is a practical subject that requires lateral thinking and it's the straight 'A' students who often struggle.

The easiest way to fail is to fall behind with the curriculum. Remember that we're learning about the human body – everything is linked. If you miss that lecture on the science behind gastric acid production the GORD workshop will leave you with a burning pain in your chest – and you won't understand why.

Keep on top of the work and you'll be fine. This means occasionally being prepared to ditch drinking games at the union for a night with your head in the books.

make friends

Whether you like it or not you're going to be stuck with that big hairy guy who picks his nose for at least the next five years. There's also a high probability that you'll end up marrying one of those drunken idiots who vomited over you during freshers week.

You've got to remember that medicine is a team sport. Refuse to play ball with your colleagues and your performance and experience will suffer. Medical school isn't a competition, you either pass or fail – and the pass mark has already been set.

It's better to drag your buddies with you when you pass the final exams rather than fall flat on your face when you attempt to go solo.

get involved

You may not be keen on chasing after a ball on the rugby pitch, or testing your tactics in the chess team but that's no excuse for not getting involved in uni activities. It's very unlikely that you won't find at least one club or society that interests you, and in that rare case you can easily set up your own.

Joining a club isn't just about improving your ball passing ability or checkmating skills, it's all about making friends and being part of university life. With the team environment of medicine and being away from home you'll need all the friends you can get. Throughout your career you'll realize that medicine is as much about who you know as what you know.

Freshers week is the time when you'll meet more potential doctors than any other. Work the crowds and get involved. Remember that students in the years above will be doctors soon. They'll be able to bail you out of trouble, not just when you're an incompetent student, but when you're an incompetent doctor and they're your boss.

a little respect

While other students will be playing with PCs we medical students get to play with people's lives. Patients are often scared, in pain and may even be terminally ill. Put yourself in their position, treat them as you would want to be treated and you won't go wrong.

Watch out for the difference between consultants who treat patients like real people and those who think they're just a piece of meat. Learn from it. By the time you finish medical school you should have a list of doctors who get the respect of both you and the patients, and a list of those who you wouldn't want to treat a member of your own family.

When you reach consultant grade you want medical students to talk about you down the pub as a 'great doctor'. That's when you'll know you've finally made it. You've got around twenty years to become this fantastic individual so start moulding yourself now.

practice makes perfect

Unlike A-levels your medical exams will test your practical skills and not just your academic knowledge. Sucking up pints down the union when you should be practicing sucking up blood may appear the better option at the time but could land you in trouble in a few years.

Sure, it's difficult trying a new practical procedure, especially when it involves sticking sharp things into little old ladies but unless you force yourself to overcome this fear now you'll struggle even more in the future – and no-one wants to be a venflon virgin forever.

Watch someone experienced first and get them to talk you through the procedure. It doesn't have to be the head of the anaesthetics department, one of your brave buddies is often a better bet as they can point out the areas where they struggled themselves.

Most medical schools and placement hospitals have a clinical skills centre where you can practice procedures. Dummies don't care if it takes seventeen tries to get an arterial blood gas sample. Ask at the centre for training workshops or times when you can practice by yourself.

Always remember that it's not just getting the needle in the vein that's important, there's going to be a terrified little old lady attached to it. You'll need to hold a conversation about her granddaughter's new baby whilst maneuvering that piece of metal in her arm.

Just like riding a bike, practical procedures become easier the more you do. You'll soon be able to simultaneously extract blood and recall all eight grandkids in order without any trouble.

staying healthy

With the emotional strain of not having mummy there to tuck you in at night and the physical strain of late nights, gallons of beer and early morning lectures your body is going to be struggling to survive. The worst thing is getting ill in the first few weeks and missing all the fun. Don't let it.

Look after yourself. Get some sleep whenever you can (preferably not in lectures). Pop those vitamin pills and down those glasses of orange juice (minus the vodka) to keep you in tip-top condition. If you're feeling run-down take a night off – its better than being stuck in bed for a week after just pushing yourself that little bit too hard.

University tutors know that students tend to be involved with activities other than molecular biology in the first few weeks, so missing the odd early morning lecture isn't going to hurt too much. Remaining alive and functioning is much more important than being able to recall DNA diagrams.

Just make sure you have a buddy you can call for help because being ill at university can be a lonely experience – and remember to look out for the signs of more serious university infections like meningitis.

You've suffered years of safe sex talks and alcohol lectures at secondary school. Well it ends here. You're an adult now and you've got to act like one. There's going to be nobody telling you that 'smoking is bad for you' and 'don't go home with strangers' any longer. It's a big bad world out there and you're in it.

On your journey to become a doctor you're going to meet thousands of people. You'll come face to face with all society's problems as soon as you walk through that hospital door each morning. It's not a curse, you're in the privileged position to see the reality and make a difference.

You know what kind of person you are. Maybe you don't drink or are already a hardened cocaine addict. Remember that now you're at university all those illicit activities are in easy reach. It's no longer as cool as sneaking a cigarette behind the bike sheds at school.

You're an adult and people expect you to behave like one. You're likely to get as much respect sticking to what you believe than being peer pressured into doing something you don't.

enjoy it

The last and most important point – enjoy it!! You're one of only six thousand students each year accepted into medical school. With electives, the best student events and an almost guaranteed job at the end, your life's looking great already. Live it up!!

GMC

The General Medical Council is the body which overseas the regulation of the UK's doctors and the medical education process. They're the ones who brand you with that all important seven digit registration number you need to practice in the UK and they can take it away too if you mess up. On their website they also publish details of the rights you have as a medical student.
www.the-gmc.org.uk/med_ed

Medical School Performance Reports

If you're interested in reading the report by the GMC Education Committee's last visit to your medical school you can check them out here. You'll be able to see what your med school is doing well and all those areas where there's 'room for improvement'. Guaranteed to make interesting reading.
www.gmc-uk.org/med_ed/visits/visits.htm

BMA

The British Medical Association publish a useful guide to being a medical student. It's got a lot of information on your rights and responsibilities. You can view it online if you've got your registration details handy, alternatively a print copy can be ordered free from the membership office.
www.bma.org.uk
T - 020 7387 4499

medical
school

**SURVIVAL
GUIDE**

**freshers
week**

get fresh

thought that a 'fresher' was a kind of fizzy sweet?? Or that you only had one 'mummy and daddy'?? Think again. Freshers week is the maddest, most fun, least slept seven days you'll have at uni.

Let's first start with the basics. Here's the translation guide you'll need to get through those first few weeks.

fresher

also known as – freshman, 'fresh' student
Similar to 'fresh milk' – innocent, unpolluted and doesn't mix well with alcohol. Refers to all new first year students. See page 24 for a guide on how to spot one. Although technically the nametag 'fresher' should only persist for those first few weeks you'll most likely be branded it for the entire first year – or longer if you're extremely incompetent and uncoordinated.

also known as - student parents
During freshers week you may be allocated a 'mummy' and/or 'daddy'. This doesn't mean you've unwittingly put yourself up for adoption. They're 'student parents' who are there to guide you through the transition into the big bad world of university life. They're great for advice on which events to go to, which clubs to join and for borrowing lecture notes and exam papers. Unlike your real mum and dad though, it's highly unlikely they'll offer to do your ironing or give you pocket money.

doing a funnel

Not exclusive to medical students but we're the only ones who understand the physiology behind it. A 'funnel' is a plastic tube (like a hosepipe) ideally less than 5cm in diameter with a funnel attached to one end. Done properly it involves crouching down, inserting the end of the plastic tube into your mouth while your rugby club

SURVIVAL
GUIDE   *medical school*

buddies pour half a crate of beer into the funnel at the other end.

Thanks to the power of gravity you'll be able to consume the same amount as the entire team in a matter of seconds. Unfortunately on most occasions it all comes pouring out again thanks to projectile vomiting or the stomach pump in your local A&E department.

Nope. It's not where you get auctioned off to the highest bidder, or a chance to ride on the merry go-round. The fresher fair is your opportunity to find out about which clubs and associations are available in your university.

There'll also be loads of big firms offering you freebies and harassing you to sign-up for bank accounts and credit cards. You'll end up leaving weighed down with free popcorn makers, CD vouchers and more bank accounts than a major international money laundering operation.

how to spot a fresher (and avoid being one)

A first year med student can be spotted more easily than a baby with chicken pox. Here's what gives you away …

1 Can be spotted fighting over free tins of beans at freshers fairs.

2 Conversation over lunch includes topics other than resection of the small bowel.

3 Jump at the chance to sign-up for clinical trials to earn a fiver being injected with the Ebola virus.

4 They turn up for all lectures – even those that aren't compulsory.

5 Commonly throw up in the tube/taxi on the way back from the union.

6 Borrow every book on pathology from the library so no 'proper' medics can use them to revise for path exams.

7 Appear to drown when trying to do a 'funnel'.

8 Clothes are badly stained with fat from the dissection lab.

9 End up on the floor after watching a surgeon make the first incision.

10 Still want to be a doctor because they 'care deeply about mankind and want to repay their debt to society for their pitiful existence'.

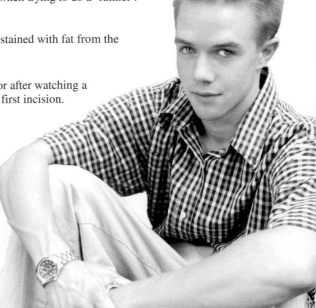

SURVIVAL GUIDE   *medical schoo*

things to join

RSM
The Royal Society of Medicine is a great organization to join if you're a medical student in London. The society is located just behind Oxford Street and student membership is £25 per year. For this, you get access to a fantastic library (which is great for revising or researching that dissertation), a fitness suite, daily lectures and events. It's also a cool place to take your mates or family for drinks as it's a really flashy inside … just make sure they dress smart.
www.rsm.ac.uk

MPS/MDU
Both the MPS and MDU are medical indemnity associations. They're there to help bail you out when things go wrong. Membership is free while you're a student and both offer great freebies. For example, the MPS offer a free textbook when you join, book and journal discounts, free quick reference learning cards and organise revision courses for finals. They also have a useful support line with can prove a life saver if you end up in a tricky legal or ethical position. Both also provide indemnity cover when you're overseas on elective.
www.mps.org.uk

BMA
The British Medical Association is the 'union' for the UK's medical doctors. They're the ones you'll see yelling and screaming on TV about doctors salaries and conditions. They'll also support you as a student if you get into arguments with the big boys at the medical school. Membership as a student is around £30 per year. For this you become a student member, receive the BMAnews weekly and the studentBMJ every month.
www.bma.org.uk

NUS
It's a bit of a bad description that the NUS is the 'national' union of students because it's not. Policy decisions about how much each university has to contribute to NUS central office have meant that many have now pulled out of this 'national' organisation. If your university still belongs to the NUS it's worth paying a few quid for a NUS card. You'll then get discounts on everything from burgers at McDonalds to CDs at Virgin and HMV.
www.nus.org.uk

MJA
Fancy yourself as the next Raj Persaud?? … or Piers Morgan?? Well there's no time like the present to put pen to paper. The Medical Journalists' Association have a special category for students interested in a career in this field. As a member you'll have the opportunity to attend workshops, press conferences and meet other more experienced writers. They also have a great mentoring program. There's a one-off cost of £10 while a student.
www.mja-uk.org

get trauma by mail

You can arrange to have '*trauma*' delivered by post four times each year.

Want to sign-up??? ... Simply complete the form below and return with payment. Your subscription will start with the next issue.

 uk edition
(4 issues per year)

£5 per year for addresses in the UK
(£10 europe, £15 world)

enter number of years
subscription required ⟶ [ ]

name _____

address _____

_____

_____

post/zip code _____

email _____

post the completed form + payment to:

> trauma subscriptions
> PO Box 36434
> London EC1M 6WA

uk pounds only. please make cheques
payable to 'trauma'

questions?? ... email us at
subscriptions@traumaroom.com

trauma

We're slightly biased here ... but trauma is the world's community of medical students and trainee doctors. We've got a presence in 27 countries from Belize to Bermuda. It's free to join our community, just sign up at www.traumaroom.com. You'll get access to discounts on everything from mobiles to textbooks and be kept up-to-date with events and medical student news in your country. You can also subscribe to 'trauma' magazine – our quarterly publication produced by medical students for medical students. It costs just £5 a year. We know you won't be able to resist so there's a subscription form opposite just waiting to be filled in. *www.traumaroom.com*

medSIN

This is a medical student non-profit organization which operates in most medical schools throughout the UK. It's part of IFMSA (International Federation of Medical Student Associations) and they run a huge number of charity projects both here and overseas. It's a society that helps you make friends, boost your CV and assist those less fortunate around the world. You can find full details of the projects available and contact details for your local medSIN group at their website. *www.medsin.org*

medical
school

**SURVIVAL
GUIDE**

*living
in halls*

moving in

You've just moved into the thirteenth floor of halls. Your room is the size of a matchbox. The person next door is playing music so loud that cracks are forming in the wall and someone is stealing your milk. Don't panic!! It's not time to move back home just yet.

Living in halls can be stressful but it's also likely to include some of the best times you'll have at medical school. Here's some tips to help you avoid hall hell.

label your food

Unless you're boarding at the university equivalent of the Ritz you're going to end up sharing a kitchen. There's nothing more irritating than finding that someone has been munching their way through your favourite pack of choccie biccies.

If you do find someone's been nicking your nosh then start initialling your grub. This way the 'I thought it was mine' argument leaves them with pie all over their face when you catch them with their fingers on yours!!

deal with disputes

If you're slowly going deaf thanks to the loud music played by your neighbour don't suffer in silence (or the lack of it), confront him. Don't shout, yell or throw your dissection scalpel. Offer him a cup of coffee, calmly explain the problem and invite him in to hear how loud the music is himself.

Unless you've moved in next to a physiology student testing his sleep deprivation thesis, there's a good chance he'll tone down his tunes. If his rocking still has you rolling around in sleepless agony get your accommodation office to pull the plug. It's their responsibility – and don't let them forget it. Mention you're considering getting the council's environmental noise team involved if they just sip their coffee while you

SURVIVAL
GUIDE   *medical school*

suffer – their licence could depend on it.

Alternatively declare all out war. *"Sounds to Annoy Your Neighbours" (CD - £14.99 iwantoneofthose.com)* is guaranteed to get him to surrender to your demands for silence.

don't shop till you drop

Cruising the aisles of your local Asda isn't the most fun activity for a Friday evening. So save yourself the torture of dragging five tons of shopping back from the supermarket by getting it to come to you. Band together with the rest of your mates on the floor and order your beer and pizzas online.

Enter your shopping list at one of the funky online supermarket sites, like *Tesco.com*, and they'll cope with your trolley trauma. As long as you request it they'll bring it right to your floor so you won't even have to change out of your PJs!!

homeless for the holidays?

Not content with making you squeeze all your belongings into a room too small to accommodate an undersized grasshopper, some halls of residence set you the extra challenge of making you move out for the holidays.

If you fail to convince them that you live in Essex, Ecuador not Essex, England and you can't possibility ship your stuff home then don't despair. American style storage centres are springing up around the country. For as little as £10 per week they provide you with a lockable storage room at one of their warehouses. Most can supply boxes and bubble wrap and offer a collection and delivery service.
www.yellowstoragecompany.com
www.selfstore.co.uk

tea for ten

The person who invented the saying 'you can't buy friends' was penniless. If you've got a few quid to spare, splashing out on a good stock of tea bags, choccie biccies and beer will give you a king-size popularity rating on your floor.

Lets face it, no cashed strapped student is going to turn down a free beer or biccie – even if you do have that personal hygiene problem. Once you've bought them over with your kindness then it's up to your personality to make that lasting impression – just pray that it'll be a good one!!

avoid teletrauma

A TV licence costs £116. Not so good, but you'll soon realise that having the distraction of mindnumbing repeats of 'Quincy' can be pretty appealing when your neighbour pops in to enlighten you on his theory of retro-fractal hexatetraelectrons.

For the record though (a) students do need a TV licence (b) pretending you only use it to watch your porn videos isn't going to stand up in court (c) students do get caught. Remember to claim back all those months you're away from halls over Christmas and summer hols. Just ask *TV Licensing* for a claim form at the end of the year.
www.tvlicensing.co.uk

can't phone a friend?

Despite 125 years to get to grips with Alexander Bell's invention of the telephone many halls of residence still haven't realised that students might want one. Somehow they figure that a network connection to entertain ourselves with free porn is more important than keeping mum and dad informed about how little they have left in their bank account.

Unlike Bell however, the net's inventers allowed for the stupidity of accommodation planners and made phone calls over the net a possibility. Now you can chat to mum in Mansfield and Auntie in Adelaide for pennies – if not free. They don't need an internet connection - just the old style phones that halls won't give you.

Don't worry if you're not a budding Bill Gates as all the kit you need, just a microphone and headset, is available in a pack from most electronic stores from £20. Invest in a webcam and you'll be able to keep track of your little bro's acne condition too.
www.net2phone.com
www.nettalk.com

Mini-fridge - Keeps your Dairylea and diet Coke cool and away from the thieving hands in the kitchen. Doubles as a mini air-conditioner in the summer. Around £40.
www.argos.co.uk

Electric Heater - In the ongoing war between students and accommodation staff you'll find the heating turned on in summer and off in winter. It defies logic. Keep warm with your own plug-in backup from £8.
www.argos.co.uk

Insurance - Lets face it, halls aren't the safest place for your belongings. You never know who has access to your room so keep your valuables locked away. Most halls of residence have insurance covering your belongings to a limit but you'll need to top this up for expensive items. Check first if you're covered on your parent's household policy.
www.saxoninsurance.com
www.endsleigh.co.uk

Laptop Lock - Everyone likes laptops because they're portable … especially thieves. It takes just a few seconds to walk away with the most expensive item in your room, along with all your course work. Don't make it easy. For less than £20 you can lock your laptop to the desk, wall or other inmovable object. Alternatively you can choose an ear-piercing alarm if it's tampered with.
www.laptopbits.co.uk

Posters - Medical students often arrive with complicated posters detailing the blood supply to the entire human body. Don't, you'll suffer bad nightmares after falling asleep looking at a dissected man on the wall. Pick up cheap fun ones from the student union 'half-price' poster sale during freshers week.

Ear Plugs - Everyone thinks that wearing ear plugs as a student is a joke. It's not. Most of the time you'll be able to cope with the extra noise that comes with living in halls, but not around exam time. Medic exams drag on longer than other subjects so while other students are partying on the floor above you'll be trying to get some shut eye. These help. Get the professional ones for club workers from most music stores.

Shower sandals - If you've got to share a bathroom. These are a must. Students traditionally aren't the cleanest members of the population and the cleaners aren't usually up to much. These help keep the dirt on the floor … not your nicely washed feet.

moving out

*j*ust when you were starting to grow attached to living in an undersized box it's time to move on. Although many universities offer medical students site accommodation for three years, most students choose to move out after the first and it's not difficult to understand why.

But the stress of seeking a new place to live can often make you wish you'd just stayed in that over-priced student prison. Here's some advice.

where to live?

Now that you've cancelled your halls contract it's time to decide on a plan. Most students opt to rent a house with their buddies, a few rent a small bedsit by themselves and others become private lodgers. You'll know which option is best for you.

Don't discount the last option as it's often overlooked. Moving in to someone else's house can be a stress free option and will help you find your feet in a new city. You might find a friendly old lady who'll do your washing and have a hot cup of cocoa ready for you before bedtime.

If you choose to band together to rent a house or flat with fellow students make sure you keep the number below five. Environmental laws get tricky past this. Also, by sacrificing the living room and turning it into an extra bedroom you can cut the weekly rent costs. Just check it's ok with the landlord first.

You've had almost a year to get to know your mates and which ones you could cope living with. Choose wisely. Your best mate's bodily functions may have been hilarious whilst you were in halls but sharing a flat with him won't be a laughing matter.

Be careful about sharing with non-med students too. As much fun as it can be to live with people who don't talk about diverticulitis over dinner you're going to have some pretty hard work ahead. They'll have easier schedules so make sure you're not the sort of person who will slack off when they do.

SURVIVAL GUIDE   *medical school*

finding a place

You've gathered together your brave bunch of potential housemates. Next step is to start the treasure hunt for that perfect student property. It's going to be a tricky task so make sure you get started early, well before you all return home for the holidays as there'll be contracts to sign.

First stop should be the university accommodation office. They publish a list of private landlords willing to rent to unruly students like yourself. Get their advice. The staff will know which ones are good landlords and who to avoid.

Ask around at uni. Students typically play 'house-musical-chairs' during the summer months. You're likely to find groups of students in the year above moving out when you want to move in. They'll know which are the good properties. If you're clever you can approach the landlord before the property is even advertised.

Loot is also worth a try. You can pick it up from most newsagents or save your cash and search online. Another good idea is to jot down your requirements on a piece of paper along with your mobile number, photocopy it and hand it in to local estate agents. They can then call you when a suitable property comes up.

If you've still had no luck. Hit the web. There's plenty of websites that allow you to search for properties to rent. We've highlighted a few that cater specifically for student accommodation – see useful resources section p35. Watch out though, many websites aren't updated regularly so you may find the property was taken months ago. *www.loot.co.uk*

checking it out

Once you've found a potential pad it's time to go check it out. Do your homework in advance. Look on a map for the location and proximity of train and bus stations. *Upmystreet.com* is useful for finding stats on everything from how often the rubbish is collected to which are the dodgy takeaways.

If you do go visiting properties don't go alone especially at night-time, and never accept a lift from a landlord. Take a friend, not just for safety but to get a second opinion too.

When you finally decide on a property go through the contract carefully. Make sure you understand the terms of the agreement and what happens if either side breaks it. Never sign anything you're unsure about. The university accommodation office or local citizen's advice bureau will be happy to talk you through it.

Next make a full inventory with the landlord. Document everything from the stains on the carpet to cutlery in the kitchen. Get it signed by both parties and witnessed. There are independent firms who will do an inventory for you. These cost around £100 but the landlord may be willing to pay part.

Remember that most disputes between students and landlords are over withheld damage deposits. A good inventory helps keep you in the clear.

If the landlord makes any promises before you move in get them in writing along with the agreed dates for completion. This way if he fails to fix the broken window or provide you with that all important microwave you've got some back-up. You might even have the right to withhold rent payments until he completes what was agreed when you signed the contract.

www.upmystreet.com

home sweet home

So the contracts are signed, the inventory is completed and you've now got fifteen huge boxes sitting in your room waiting to be unpacked. The last thing before you relax is to 'break-in' your fellow housemates to their new environment.

Get the ground rules sorted early. If you're the type of house that need to work out a 'cleaning rota' then get it sorted. You're going to need to be flexible towards your new housemates the first couple of weeks but things should slowly come together.

There are bound to be things that will start to irritate you during the year. Try and stay calm. Toenail biting isn't the most pleasant quality in a housemate but it's not worth losing a friend over.

If you do have problems don't let them drag on. The university accommodation office is there to help with a dodgy landlord or even dodgier flatmates. In most cases though you're likely to just have a great hassle-free year.

All that's left to do is enjoy your new found freedom and plan for that obligatory house-warming party – just remember that you've signed the inventory so keep all extra carpet stains to a minimum.

iammoving.com
One of the worst things about moving is having to notify all the banks, credit card and mobile phone companies of your new address. You can spend days with the phone glued to your ear listening to reruns of Abba's greatest hits. Don't, this rather cool website will notify all those companies for you just by ticking a few boxes. You even get a reward of a free Domino's pizza just for doing so – it's worth moving house every year just for that.
www.iammoving.com

University of London Accommodation Office
This site is packed with useful information even if you don't live in the nation's capital. Whether you're looking for a property checklist to tick off when quizzing landlords or a handy budget planner you'll find it here. There's also a 'flatmate finder' if you're searching in London.
www.housing.lon.ac.uk

Bunk
Want to check out what your new halls of residence has on offer, or whether you should be moving to another campus?? This site allows you to compare the accommodation facilities at over 240 UK universities and colleges.
www.bunk.com

upmystreet.com
If you're not too clued up about a new area then check out this web site. It'll provide you with a great insight into your new postcode, from crime rates to the nearest 24hr convenience store. The community discussion board is a great way to find out what the current residents think of an area and for recommendations on the best Chinese takeaway.
www.upmystreet.com

Accommodation for Students
Looking for student-style accommodation?? ... then look no further. This search engine allows to key in your preferences and provides you with a time-saving list of properties in your chosen region. There's also useful information about typical rents in each area and a flatmate search feature.
www.accommodationforstudents.com

medical
school

SURVIVAL
GUIDE

money

cashing in

medical school can be an expensive place. There's new textbooks to buy, your rent is due, mobile phone bill needs paying ... and there's all that money you desperately want to donate to the student union bar.

Here's some advice to keep those pounds securely in your pocket.

balls to budgets

You could work out your weekly spend on travel, split your yearly book purchases down to a monthly basis and calculate how many pints of milk you can afford every twelve months but is it really going to help?? Probably not. Unless your life is so dull that one week is no different than the next forget the micro-economics and stick to basic money management.

Let your bank do all the calculations you need. They'll tell you how much you spend each month – just look for the 'Total out' on your next statement. Then divide your total yearly income by twelve. If you've spent more than your monthly budget then you've got to cut back by that amount next month or make up the difference through part-time work.

Many students start fretting over finances and about getting into debt but stacking up the loans is all part of being a medical student. Remember that we've got six years of study and little time for part-time work. The good news is that we're handed a well paid job at the end.

If you do need help with your cash crisis there's plenty of assistance on offer. The first stop should be the student union welfare office or the support section of your university. They'll be able to work through a plan to get you back in the black.

current accounts

Banks scramble to sign-up new med students at freshers fairs. But don't just be tempted by the offer of a free popcorn maker, make sure the provider you choose is practical too. Remember that as a medical student you can be posted to far-flung hospitals in the middle of nowhere. You'll want a bank that has branches in all major towns and a card that can be used in most cashpoints without a charge.

All banks offer student packages but some are better than others. *Smile* (part of the *Royal Bank of Scotland*) have a special student current account offering a high interest rate on that cashed student loan cheque while you're waiting to spend it. It's an internet bank too so you'll be able to check why your card was refused at the bar when you return home from the union at 3am.

Also, take a glance at the overdraft allowances and interest rates. There's a big difference even between the big four high street banks. It may be worth asking if they offer 'Professional Studies Loans' (see page 40) at this stage if you think you might need one as you're more likely to be accepted if you've been with a bank for a few years.

credit cards

"Never ever borrow money on a credit card even if you have to go homeless, starve or miss out on a free popcorn maker," they tell you. In reality though most students collect credit cards like football stickers. There are benefits to plastic cash just as long as you're wary.

Most companies now offer interest free incentives to sign-up. These can be great to get through to your next loan cheque. Hopping from one card to another every six months is fine say experts – it's not going to affect your credit rating. Just be careful as you may not get a high enough limit to cover your old balance.

Also look out for cards offering up to 1% cashback (or 2% promotional) on your purchases. Pay for your college residence fees by card upfront and you'll get a nice 70 quid cashback for your effort (fees = 3500 pounds at 2% promotional).

Buying all the recommended textbooks throughout the medical course can leave you with a budget deficit the size of a small developing nation. So don't. You'll soon learn not to buy the first book the lecturer tells you (especially ones they've written themselves).

Borrowing from the library is an obvious solution. Remind yourself a week before the start of a new module to reserve all the books you'll need. This will save you from the scrum that develops amongst the shelves straight after the first lecture. If they don't have the book you're looking for most libraries will be happy to order it for you.

Some books you'll want to buy, but there's no reason to buy brand new copies. Second hand books are normally advertised around campus. You can also sell/buy used books on *Amazon.co.uk* and on the pinboard section of the *traumaroom.com* site. If you're lucky you'll find notes made by previous students of important points, exam hints and which lecturers you need to avoid.

A few high street booksellers like Blackwells and Waterstones offer buy-back options for used books at some stores.
www.amazon.co.uk
www.traumaroom.com

professional studies loans

First the basics, a professional studies loan is designed to support you through your studies. Most high street banks offer them as special packages for medical and law students who are seen as better future customers. You can borrow up to £20,000 and this can be at a fixed or flexible interest rate.

You'll begin repayments usually nine months after you qualify. Shop around and get written quotes. A number of students have found that a certain high-street bank added extra 'administration charges' to the agreed quotes. Ask for a written copy of the rates and the total repayable along with all charges.

The BMA offer a professional studies loan in association with Natwest so it must be the best for medical students?? ... Wrong. Even though it's got the BMA's name attached to it you can get better deals from some of the other high street banks – so shop around.

hardship help

For some students the financial demands of medical school are going to be more difficult than for others. If you're finding it tough there's always help out there if you know where to look. Most universities have hardship funds that can be accessed by those struggling with the basics. The first stop should be the student union or university welfare team.

Your local education authority is also worth a try. In many cases they may be able to reimburse you for travel expenses incurred as part of the course – which can add up to quite a bit.

Don't let things get out of hand. If you're finding yourself on a downward financial

student discounts

You're special being a student and they even give you a card to prove it. This little piece of plastic is your key to discounts, free ice-cream and other pleasures. Here's a little taster.

Topshop/Topman
Burtons/Dorothy Perkins
10 per cent discount
London Transport Travelcards
30 per cent on weekly, monthly and annual cards (yearly £5 processing fee for Photocard)
Rymans
10 per cent discount on all stationery
Pizza Hut
20 per cent off between Sunday and Thursday - for dine-in, takeaway and delivery orders (excludes buffet)
HMV
10 per cent discount in store + online
www.hmv.co.uk/students
Virgin Megastore
10 per cent discount
Habitat
10 per cent discount
McDonalds
Free hamburger, cheeseburger or McFlurry with any Extra Value Meal *or* free sausage/bacon and egg McMuffin with any Breakfast Value Meal
Vodafone
10 per cent discount on monthly bill
Dominos Pizza
10 per cent discount
Jessops
10 per cent discount on camera supplies
Peacocks
10 per cent discount
Dolland & Aitchison
Free eye test and 25 per cent discount
London Theatres
Stand-by tickets available to students

about an hour before performance. Prices from £10 available at the box office
Microsoft
Huge discounts on software licences, including all the Office packages
www.microsoft.com/uk/education
Student Railcard
1/3 off most rail fares
Cheap Flights
Available for under 25s. May need to purchase an additional ISIC card
www.studentflights.co.uk
www.statravel.co.uk
Cinemas
as advertised

www.
traumaroom
.com

But where's the discounts on medical stuff?? ... Simple. Sign up at *traumaroom.com* for your unique ID. This gives you access to up to 30 per cent off medical textbooks, equipment and courses. It only takes a few minutes and gives you full access to the 'trauma' community site too.

spiral ask for some advice. In the long term you'll be glad you did.

spend, spend, spend

So you're feeling better now. You've got your current account, cards, student loan, professional studies loan and enough credit to buy a small mansion. It may be reassuring that you've got all this cash at your fingertips but try to think long-term.

When you start earning do you really want to use your salary to make repayments while you continue to live on a diet of baked beans and pot noodles?? Sure, loans are there to make life easier in the meantime but don't get carried away. It's much better to keep control of your finances now and then splash out on that convertible sports car when you start your first job.

So what happens if you're one of the lucky people who have cash left over?? Maybe you have an extra student loan that you don't need, or went tea-total last month and saved a small fortune. No matter how much cash you've got don't let it sit there doing nothing, make it work just as hard as you do.

Dargan Miller, a student financial advisor offers an alternative to donating all that extra cash to the student bar –

Find a high-interest savings account
There's no point keeping your cash in your current account says Miller. "Once you've budgeted ahead for the next few months keep the extra cash in a high interest savings account," he advises. "You can get over 4 per cent interest and still have instant access to your money."

Egg	4.0 per cent	www.egg.com
Cahoot	4.27 per cent	www.cahoot.co.uk
ING	4.5 per cent	www.ingdirect.co.uk

correct as of 26th April 2004

Premium Bonds
Think you're a lucky person? Yes. Then maybe you should consider premium bonds. Run by the government, there's a number of advantages explains Miller, "Firstly, you never lose money as you can surrender your bonds at any time and get back what you paid. Secondly, all your winnings are tax-free. Finally, it's fun and safer than playing the lottery."
www.nationalsavings.co.uk

SURVIVAL GUIDE *medical school*

ISAs and Shares

If you've got a serious amount of money it might be worth considering other options. "Only get involved in the more risky investments such as shares and ISAs if you can afford too," advises Miller. "Don't let it jeopardise your education as this is the best investment you'll make. You'll need at least two thousand pounds to make it worthwhile as the costs of buying and selling shares make any profit on smaller amounts unlikely."

As with all financial decisions Miller suggests you get professional advice before choosing whether to invest in shares, savings or shots of vodka at the student union bar.

money, money, money

So all you've got now to look forward too is six years of *Tesco's* value baked beans and king size *Pot Noodles*. But while you're staring into that empty plate feeling hungry here's something to cheer you up.

Below are the current doctor's pay bandings for the first year after qualification. They're likely to change by the time you pass finals but at least you have some idea of the going rate. Now you can dream about what you're going to spend it on first.

Band	Salary
1	19,185
1C	23,022
1B	26,859
1A	28,778
2	20,420
2B	30,630
2A	36,756
3	43,310

Correct April 2004

Most PRHOs are on banding 2A or 2B at present.

Let's be honest. Medicine is a tough course but we've still got plenty of time for a bit of part-time work. When you add up all that time you spend watching EastEnders and the afternoons you bunk off those path lectures it's enough to help prop up your bank balance. Here's some options.

Medical Secretary
Pay –   Around 7 pounds per hour.
Qualifications – Good typing speed. Able to spell big words like 'Klienfelters'.
Good points – Easy to find. Easy to do.
Bad points – Mind-numbingly boring.
www.fairstaff.com
www.lifeline-personnel.com

Medical Journalism
Pay – Up to 75 pounds per article.
Qualifications – B abel to right beter than this.
Good points – Looks good on your CV. Get to see your name in print.
Bad points – You need a little talent otherwise all your hard work may never get published.
www.studentbmj.com/contact/writing.html

Nursing Assistant
Pay – Depends on shifts. Around 7-15 pounds per hour.
Qualifications – Some patient experience.
Good points – Good for picking up the odd medical fact.
Bad points – You already know some of the things nurses have to do.

Sperm Donor
Pay – Technically it's your 'expenses' only. Typically up to 25 pounds a time.
Qualifications – Male.
Good points – Job satisfaction.
Bad points – Difficult line of work if you're female.
Local clinics – Check Yellow Pages.

Support For Learning
Fantastic up-to-date site detailing all the financial stats you could need. Find out which is the best student bank account with all the rates and freebies listed. They also have information about professional studies loans and a comprehensive database of grants and awards.
www.supportforlearning.org.uk/money

Educational Grants Advisory Service
A national body that brings together all the grants, scholarships and access funds in a simple, searchable format. They also offer a telephone and face-to-face support service for students whose financial situation threatens the continuation of their studies.
www.egas-online.org.uk

Student Loans Company
Student loans sound simple in theory but the reality is all in the small print. It's worth taking a look at the different limits that are available along with the current interest rates. You'll also be able to work out how large a chunk of your doctors salary they'll be taking when you start to pay them back.
www.slc.co.uk

UKCOSA
If you're an overseas student then this website lists charitable trusts and organisations that provide grants and scholarships specifically for you. It's also packed with useful information on everything from immigration hassles to part-time employment rights.
www.ukcosa.org.uk

NUS
Still not sorted on student finance?? Then the NUS website contains all the datasheets, information and resources you could need. It's easily indexed and available to you even if you're not an NUS member. While you're there check out all the other benefits open to you as a student.
www.nusonline.co.uk

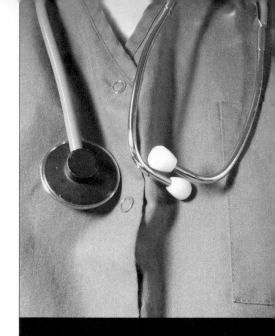

medical
school

SURVIVAL
GUIDE

starting

clinicals

ward work

no sooner have you learnt that the heart doesn't look the shape of the ones on Valentines cards than they set you loose in a hospital to find a real one.

Hitting the wards for the first time can be as terrifying as visiting the zoo as a little kid. You stroll around viewing the strange species in the cubicles on either side trying not to look scared.

The chief zookeeper (the consultant) is on patrol. You feel lost. Nobody has explained all the simple questions, and you're too frightened to ask. But don't go running away with your tail between your legs just yet. Here's all the answers you'll need to be top monkey.

do I wear a white coat?

If you're a practical type of person you'll find white coats a great idea – there's plenty of pockets to hold stethoscopes, mobile phones and tuna sandwiches. Otherwise, unless the consultant objects most students don't wear one.

There's a number of reasons for this (a) it's extra washing to do (b) you'll probably forget to take it anyway (c) it's way too hot in the summer (d) despite thinking that it might make you look like a real doctor people just confuse you with a phlebotomist or hospital cleaner (e) there's no proven health benefit to the patient anyway.

what should I take with me on the ward?

A stethoscope
Vital. Placing your ear directly on a women's chest is likely to get you chucked out of medical school pretty quick. Don't buy an expensive one because you'll hear lots of extra noises that only a specialist cardiovascular consultant will understand. One at around £50 is sufficient.

Pentorch
Not just useful for finding dropped keys on the way home from the union. It's needed for all neurological examinations.

SURVIVAL GUIDE *medical school*

A Good Pen

This is a decent ball point to write in the patient's notes. Don't ever use a fountain pen as it will smudge and you'll get a smack around the ear from the consultant.

A pocketful of cheap biros

Once you reach registrar level there's an unwritten rule that you just borrow pens from other people and never give them back. Keep this stock away from your good set.

Name badge and ID card

You'll lose these numerous times during the five-year course. A handy tip is to attach your ID badge to your stethoscope, this way you might be lucky enough to get your stethoscope back if you lose it. Alternatively if you've upset the nurses enough you'll probably have lost both forever.

Books

You'll see some medical students struggling round with a pile of books heavier than their own body weight. Don't, all you need is a comprehensive pocket-sized book to sneakily look up the answers when the consultant's back is turned. A good option is the *'Cheese and Onion'* otherwise known as the *'Oxford Handbook of Medicine'*.

If you feel a lightweight with just this a good addition is the *'trauma On The Ward Survival Guide'*. Although we're a little biased, it explains in idiot-proof language step-by-step guides to all the examinations and procedures you'll have to perform – great for having a quick check before you go see a patient.

what does 'on take' mean?

This means that your firm (the medical/surgical unit of consultant, registrar, SHO and PRHO) are the team accepting all new hospital admissions that come through A&E that day. A firm is usually 'on take' no more than once a week.

Clerking patients on these days in A&E is one of the most useful and fun parts of being a medical student. It also gives you a chance to practice some minor procedures like taking blood, suturing and cannulation – which makes you feel useful rather than just getting in the way.

Be careful though, clerking patients 'on take' means you'll probably have to present to the consultant on the post-take ward round which can be very early the next morning!!

---

medical student

Duration	5-6 years
Role	To be humiliated.
How to identify	Can be seen hiding behind curtains, tables and big textbooks to avoid being spotted.

---

prho

Duration	1 year
Role	Secretary, telephone answering service and general slave.
How to identify	Can be located by following the continuous bleeping sound emitted from a small box attached to their waist.

---

sho

Duration	2-3 years
Role	They don't even know. They're trapped between knowing nothing and being expected to know everything.
How to identify	Look out for stressed, tired, angry people with stethoscopes.

---

registrar

Duration	5-6 years
Role	The last hope before having to call the consultant back from the golf course.
How to identify	They look cool, calm and knowledgeable after the trauma of their SHO years but when the consultant asks a difficult question watch them fall apart!!

---

consultant

Duration	Forever. They never die – they live on in the nightmares of medical students and doctors everywhere.
Role	The answer to all our prayers when things go wrong, and the person who makes us feel wrong when things go right.
How to identify	Surrounded by a bright white light and followed by a trail of angels who open doors for him. The one everyone refers to as 'God' or 'God, he's coming where are those blood results'.

---

those big blue things

They're called nurses. Warning – Be nice to them!! If you think the wrath of a consultant is bad just wait to see what a staff nurse with a bedpan can do. As a medical student or junior doctor they can make your job ten times easier ... or damn near impossible!!

There are different varieties. They start with student nurses (who you will feel sorry for – their life is even worse than ours!!) and then become staff nurses. This group have letters after their grade to explain how senior they are. Finally charge nurses are the ones to be afraid of, they're the ones who get to boss everyone around. Don't mess with them!!

There's a new variety called Specialist nurses. They can do some of the tasks of doctors and are really useful if you need someone to show you how to suture or do some other procedure without having to ask your house officer.

If you do ever manage to upset one of the nurses, even if it's their fault, make sure you apologise. Just trust us on this one!! Offer to go make them a cup of coffee, or if the worst comes to the worst, a 'thank you for all your help' box of chocolates. You won't regret it next time you need a favour.

---

what is a 'grand round'?

Usually occurs once a week when a consultant or visiting speaker give a talk or present a patient. Doctors turn up because they need it signed up for their records. You'll turn up for the free lunch or because you need somewhere dark to sleep off your hangover.

what is a 'venflon' or 'cannula'?

It's a little tube which is inserted into a vein usually on the back of the hand or somewhere on the forearm. It's taped in place so it can be used to administer drugs or fluids at a later date.

There's a needle in it to help pierce the skin but this is removed once the tube has been inserted. It's not uncomfortable for the patient and can be left in place for up to five days. The overall procedure is called 'cannulation'.

what is a 't.t.a.'?

It means to 'to take away'. When patients leave hospital, doctors fill out a 'TTA' form which details their diagnosis, any medications they still need and a future treatment plan. One copy stays in the patient's notes, another gets sent to the GP and the patient gets a third copy.

Doctors often dread filling out these forms, especially for patients with lots of complaints. Get a good look at them while a medical student as you'll be expected to complete hundreds as a junior doctor.

what is the 'mess'?

This is where the junior doctors 'hang out' or hide from the consultant. The doctor's mess is funded (in part) by the hospital and facilities vary immensely. In some hospitals you'll find satellite TV and pool tables, while in others it'll just be plastic chairs and a few lockers.

The mess is also a great place for medical students to pass the time between the morning ward round and being allowed home. You'll have to convince one of the docs to give you the door combination first though.

what is a 'drug lunch'?

In the UK drug companies aren't allowed to advertise directly to patients so they concentrate all their efforts on the docs. They hope the next time a new patient presents with angina the doctor will prescribe their branded drug costing many times more than the generic version.

Unfortunately for them, doctors are quite cynical and don't have enough time to let any drug advertising sink in. So the drug companies 'buy' time with doctors by sponsoring lunches. In return for providing an array of free sandwiches, drinks and snacks they get a few minutes to boast about their new wonder drug.

And we med students get to benefit too. We can turn up, tuck into all the free food then sleep through the rest of the meeting – just make sure the talk isn't on a gruesome surgical procedure otherwise those sandwiches might not stay down for long.

abbrevia-what?

Hospitals are designed to be complicated. All the abbreviations and long names help make the patient feel stupid and make the doctors look intelligent. So if you don't want to look like a member of the public here's some of the key terms to know –

Administration of Drugs - OD (once daily), **OM** (each morning), **BD** (twice daily), **TDS** (three times daily), **QDS** (four times daily), **PC** (after food), **nocte** (at night)
ALTS - Advanced Trauma Life Support
Barrier Nurse - Nursing an infectious patient in isolation. Usually in a side room.
BNF - British National Formulary - Essential book describing all medications that can be prescribed. Should be available on every ward.
CABG (pronounced Cabbage) - Coronary Artery Bypass Graft
CCU - Coronary Care Unit - Specialist unit offering more intensive treatment for acute coronary cases.
CHD - Coronary Heart Disease
CMHT - Community Mental Health Team - eg. psychiatric nurses, social workers
CT - Computer Tomography (kind of scan)
DNA - Did not Attend
D&V - Diarrhoea and Vomiting
ECT - ElectroEncephalograph - Recording of brain wave patterns
Elective Admission - A pre-arranged admission
FP10 - Prescription Form
HDU - High Dependency Unit - Care for patients who need extra care but are not critical enough for ITU.
IM - Intramuscular
ITU/ICU - Intensive Therapy/Care Unit
IV - Intravenous
MIU - Minor Injuries Unit
MRI - Magnetic Resonance Image (another kind of scan)
NFA - No Fixed Address
OPD - Outpatient Department
OT - Occupational Therapist
PO - Orally
PR - Rectally
SCBU - Special Care Baby Unit
SRN - Registered nurse

Soon you'll be swinging your stethoscope round your neck and venturing into the big bad world of hospital life. Here's how to look both cool and clever with the help of a professional image consultant.

imagine this

When your consultant can't distinguish you from an RTA victim that's been trailed through an articulated lorry sideways, there's a problem. "Image is everything," says **Deborra Radcliffe**, a professional image consultant. "Looking smart and dressing professionally can actually make you appear more intelligent than you actually are."

male magic

"For men, wear a shirt and tie that complement each other with the same colour shades," suggests Radcliffe. If you've less colour sense than a blind patient without a guide dog, high street chains such as *Next* and *Debenhams* sell pre-packaged matching combinations. "Shirts with cufflinks will improve your ranking but only if you wear a jacket or white coat on top." *Pokemon* ties are only acceptable if you're doing paeds … or if your consultant has the mental age of a five-year-old.

winning as a woman

If you're a woman, forget the skirt advises Radcliffe, "Women who power dress are taken more seriously." For women who have a soft voice and mild manner, wear darker colours to appear more confident. "Students who ooze confidence should choose paler shades to help you take advantage of your womanly side – it will make you appear more in touch with the patient's perspective."

role play

Making small talk with a patient about haemorrhoids can often put you in more pain than they are. The fear of talking to someone for the first time is all about being scared of the unexpected suggests Radcliffe. "Having a practised introduction when you meet a new patient can help you through this difficult period," she advises. "The first 30 seconds of conversation is the most stressful and yet the most important for making a positive impression." Practice your speech and facial expressions in front of a mirror, Radcliffe proposes.

escaping embarrassment

Examining semi-naked patients can be an uncomfortable experience even for the most confident. You need to distance yourself from the reality of the situation suggests

Radcliffe. "There's nothing unnatural about nakedness – it's just the human emotions we've attached to it," she explains. "Treating the consultation in a purely clinical way is one way to deal with this. Removing the concept of the 'person' from the 'body' often works."

your patient

CARDIOVASCULAR SYSTEM
RESPIRATORY
ABDOMEN
NEUROLOGICAL
MUSCULO - SKELETAL

now that you've got a shiny new stethoscope round your neck, a tendon hammer in pocket and butterflies in your stomach it's time to go see your first patient. It's a nerve-wracking experience but after a little practice you'll soon find taking histories as easy as making a shopping list. Here's some useful tips.

don't go it alone

Taking a buddy with you when you see a patient isn't so that they can laugh at your mistakes afterwards, it's a great way to improve your history taking technique. Watching how someone else interacts with a patient and getting feedback on your own performance is a rapid way to work out where you're going right and wrong.

You'll also find in those early days that the struggle to ask questions and take notes is often too confusing. Having a buddy there to transcribe while you talk lets you concentrate on one thing at a time. Once you've mastered the art of articulating your questions then start trying to note it down.

acing that intro

Plucking up the courage to go speak to a patient is a stage we all go through. It's useful to remember that most patients have spent days stuck on the wards. They're usually more than happy to chat to a cheerful medical student about their grandchildren, experiences of the war and, if you pressure them, their bronchitis.

Here's a few standard introductions which could prove useful if you get tongue-tied at the bedside –

"Hello, my name is Joe. I'm a final year medical student with Dr. Smith. I was wondering if you could spare half an hour for me to ask you some questions about your medical history. It would be very useful as part of my training."

SURVIVAL GUIDE *medical school*

"If you feel tired at any time or don't want to continue just let me know and we can end it there."

"Are you comfortable?? Do you mind if I sit here??"

Ensuring the patient is as comfortable and relaxed as possible is as much for your benefit as theirs. An uncomfortable and anxious patient isn't likely to divulge those personal facts you'll be seeking. Always be aware of their privacy too.

getting the facts

Keep your questions as 'open' as possible and let the patient do the talking. A phrase such as "Starting from the very beginning, tell me the reason you came into hospital" will help set you on the right track. If you're lucky the patient will tell you everything you need to know.

'Closed questions' are useful to keep the interview moving in the right direction and to pick up those details that the patient has overlooked. A good tip is to list the main headers for the history on a piece of paper before you see the patient. A quick glance down will let you know which questions you still need to cover.

Make sure you establish the real reason for the patient's stay in hospital. Many will happily talk for hours about their hernia, but fail to mention the double decker bus which hit them last Saturday and the four hours of surgery that ensued.

A good way to make sure you have the information correct is to summarise back to the patient what they have told you. You'll often be surprised how easy it is to interpret things wrongly. It's better for the patient to point out your mistakes than the consultant on the early morning ward round.

putting it on paper

When making notes use the patient's own words to describe events and symptoms. Keep it jargon free and summarise wherever possible without omitting important details. Try to keep the events in order otherwise it's easy to get confused when it comes to presenting your findings.

We haven't enough space in this book to talk through the entire history and examination, but we've included a sample history and examine write-up on the next few pages. This will hopefully be a useful guide on which to base your write-up after the interview.

Medical student clerking - Joe Bloggs   18th June, 2004

Johnathan Smith
DOB - 17.06.29

75   ♂   Caucasian   Retired Bus Driver
         Self-admission via casualty on Saturday, October 18.

PC -   Shortness of Breath

HPC -   Brought in by friends 12.10am Saturday
         1/52 Hx of shortness of breath at rest. Worse at night. Wakes up breathless.
         Sleeps with 3 pillows. Last two nights acutely short of breath so slept
         upright in chair.
         Associated with -
         (1) Productive "deep chesty" cough. Produces tablespoon of clear/"frothy" sputum
         daily. No fresh blood present.
         (2) Night sweats
         Reduced exercise tolerance to <10m
         No previous episodes prior to admission
         RS - °wheeze, °chest pain, °hx of asthma, °recent foreign travel °recent
         chest infections
         CVS - patient has noticed mild ankle swelling °sob on exertion, °hx of ischaemic
         heart disease/lvf
         Risk factors - Smokes 10/day. (30 day up to age 65), postive FH

PMH -   Osteoarthritis - operation on L hand 1992
         °epilpsy/cva/mi/hypertension/tb/asthma/diabetes

DH -   Coproxamol - 2 tablets PRN
         Hydrocortisone cream - topically PRN
         °reported drug allergies

FH -   Father - died after "many heart attacks" age 67. Heavy smoker.
         Mother - died from "old age" age 98. No medical problems.
         Brother - Severe angina. Age 72.

SH -   Lives alone. First floor. One flight of stairs.
         Completely independent and mobile. Enjoys walking.
         Good support network of friends and family.
         Smoked 30/day up until 65. Still smokes 10/day.
         Non-drinker

ROS -   General - °weight change. Appetite good. Usually sleeps well.
         GI - °vomiting/nausea/indigestion/dysphagia. Bowels regular. No blood PR.
         °constipation/diarrhoea
         GU - °incontinence/dysuria/haematuria/nocturia
         NS - °dizziness/ataxia/headaches/weakness

<u>O/E</u>

General   Appeared comfortable at rest. Alert and orientated in time, place and person.
°jaundice/anaemia/clubbing/cyanosis/lymphadenopathy
Temperature - 36.8°C

CVS   Pulse 80/min. Regular.
BP - 130/80
JVP - Mildly elevated
Bilateral pedal oedema

Apex beat - 5th intercostal, mid-clavicular
°precordial thrills/parasternal heaves
°scars/chest deformities

HS - I —— II + 0

Peripheral pulses

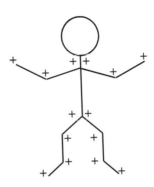

RS   Respiratory rate 18/min. Regular.
Trachea central.
Chest expansion equal and symmetrical

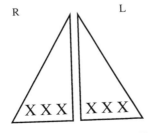

Bilateral basal crepitations

°expiratory/inspiratory wheeze

No sputum sample available

GIS

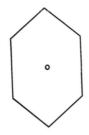

Abdomen soft, non-tender
Non-distended
°masses/scars/visible veins

LSKK non-palpable
Bowel sounds normal
Genitalia/hernial orifices - not examined
PR - not performed

NS   Cranial nerves

I	Not formally tested
II	Vision normal with glasses
	Fundi not examined
III/IV/VI	Pupils equal. React to light and accommodation
	Extra ocular movements normal
V	°diplopia/nystagmus
	Corneal refles not tested
VII	°facial weakness
VIII	Not formally tested
IX	Gag reflex not formally tested
X	Palate elevation central and equal
XI	Accessory muscles normal
XII	Tongue protrusion equal and central

PNS   °tremor/wasting/fasiculations

	R	L
Upper Limb		
Tone	n	n
Power	5/5	5/5
Co-ordination	n	n
Sensation	n	n
Upper Limb		
Tone	n	n
Power	5/5	5/5
Co-ordination	n	n
Sensation	n	n

Reflexes	BJ	+	+
	SJ	+	+
	TJ	+	+
	KJ	not elicited	+
	AJ	+	+
	PR	+	+

| Gait | Normal |

Your challenge now is to turn the ramblings of your patient into a succinct summary of the main points for the consultant. No-one is expecting you to master this first time and it may take months or years before you become proficient.

A useful tip is to write it out as you intend to say it. This will help with the nerves and allow you to order it in your head. Gradually however, you'll need to learn how to present directly from the notes you've scribbled down at the bedside.

Find out from the SHO in advance whether the consultant will expect you present a summary of a few lines or a more comprehensive account of the patient's history.

Here's an example of the case history on the previous pages –

"This is Mr Smith. A 75 year old retired bus driver who was brought to A&E by friends with shortness of breath on Saturday. He has a one week history of progressively worsening breathlessness. Sleeps with three pillows and wakes frequently. Currently needs to sleep in chair. He reports night sweats and a "dry, chesty" productive cough with approx a tablespoon of clear frothy sputum per day. No haemoptysis is present. His exercise tolerance is reduced to <10m.

He reports no previous episodes and no precipitating factors. He has had no recent chest infections, foreign travel or history of asthma.

For risk factors he smokes 10 per day, previously 30 up to the age of 65. His father had "multiple heart attacks" and his brother aged 72 suffers from severe angina. His only other past medical problem is osteoarthritis affecting his feet and hands.

He is currently taking coproxamol and topical hydrocortisone as required. He reported no drug allergies.

He lives alone on first floor but is independent and mobile. Appears to have a good support network of friends. He is a non-drinker.

On review of systems there was nothing further of note.

On examination he appeared comfortable at rest. He was aprexial and their were no signs of jaundice, anaemia, clubbing, cyanosis or lymphadenopathy. His pulse was regular at 80 minute. His BP was 130/80 and his JVP was mildly raised.

On examination of his cardiovascular system his apex beat was undisplaced and there were no signs of any thrills or heaves. His heart sounds were normal with no additional sounds auscultated. His peripheral pulses were all present. Bilateral pedal oedema was present.

His respiratory rate was 18/min and regular. Chest movements were equal and symmetrical and his trachea was non-displaced. On auscultation I could hear bilateral basal crepitations however the rest of his lungs were clear. No wheeze was present.

Abdomen was soft and non-tender. There was no evidence of any masses, scars or distension. No organomegaly was present. Bowel sounds were normal. I did not exam his genitalia or perform a PR.

His cranial nerves appeared grossly intact and peripheral nervous system appeared normal. Tone, power, co-ordination and sensation were normal. Reflexes were normal although I could not elicit a knee-jerk response on his right side. His gait was normal.

A Practical Guide to Clinical Examination
Taking a history and examining a patient for the first time can be a difficult experience. This site is a comprehensive guide to examination of all the systems of the body with text, anatomical links, pictures and video. It also includes sections on 'presenting your findings' and 'putting it all together'. Totally invaluable.
medicine.ucsd.edu/clinicalmed/introduction.htm

Tomorrow's Doctors
Remember that you're not expected to qualify from medical school competent in open heart surgery. It's useful to have a look at the types of skills and procedures you'll be expected to be able to perform by the time you finish final year. The list can be found, along with other useful stuff, at the GMC's Tomorrow's Doctors site.
www.gmc-uk.org/med_ed/tomdoc.htm

medical
school

**SURVIVAL
GUIDE**

*passing
the exams*

top marks

You thought A-levels were difficult? Or maybe counting change in Tesco was your limit? It doesn't matter anymore, you made it to medical school – but it isn't time to relax just yet. Those never ending exams just keep coming. Here's some tips to help you pass.

trust no-one

The first and most important rule about exams is to trust no-one but yourself. Students in the year above are likely, in their rose tinted, beer-fueled nostalgia to recount heroic tales of having done only two hours work to pass all their pre-clinical exams. While on the other hand your own year colleagues are more likely to terrify you with the amount of revision they have done.

Only you know how much work you need to do. Remember, now that you've have passed A-levels you're an accomplished exam taking machine and should be familiar with your abilities and exam technique.

during the year

Try to go to all the lectures and teaching sessions. Nobody will blame you for missing the occasional dull lecture but good attendance will impress the examiners if your exam performance is marginal. If you do miss a session photocopy your mates notes now and make sure you understand them, don't leave it till exam time.

Get to know your lecturers and tutors and ask them questions. It's often very difficult to ask questions in a packed lecture theatre, but as they always say, if you have the guts to ask the question there'll be another 20 people who didn't understand but were too frightened to ask.

Don't be afraid to approach fellow students or your second year mums and dads for help if you're struggling. They're often much better at explaining a complicated subject as they probably had difficulties grasping the same topic too.

past papers

Medical students are inherently lazy. A quality that doesn't disappear once you get to slap 'Dr' in front of your name – or Dean for that matter. Like us, the big boys who run our universities like to take shortcuts whenever they can and this includes setting exams.

By simply rewording, or blatantly copying and pasting previous questions the exam setter saves themselves enough time for an extra round of golf. More importantly it gives you the opportunity to pick up extra marks.

Armed with reams of past exams papers some students can become notoriously secretive about their past paper stash. Hunting them down is a valid exam revision activity and a great excuse for a night down the union after a hard day of hitting the books. This is where all those 'friends' you inadvertently made in the drunken haze of freshers week have their use.

If your friends have no papers, or you simply have no friends, don't despair. You're likely to find at least a few years worth of exam material in the library, on the web or from tutors (if you beg hard enough). Failing that all universities set similar exam questions and formats (especially those that make up the *University of London* board) so there's plenty of opportunity to hunt down at least a few papers at other uni's too.

top-up tutorials

When the only thing you learnt during your immunology module was the telephone number for the *'The Wright Stuff'* support line you (a) obviously have been spending more time watching TV than attending lectures (b) are very lucky that you can actually receive channel 5 (c) may need that number soon as the exams are now only weeks away.

So with just two weeks to a potential 'kicked-out-of-medical-school' exam it's time to get your act together. At exam time most tutors become all sympathetic and helpful to us poor little med students. It's quite easy to persuade them to leave their electrophoresis plates to electrophorese themselves and offer emergency, last minute, 'all-you-need-to-know' style tutorials.

Asking for a 'group tutorial' with some of your mates is the best way to persuade them. This makes them feel extra special and removes the perceived threat of you hitting on them whilst you're gazing over petri dishes late at night.

Make sure they stick to the important exam stuff. Better still, give them a list of topics so they can plan the time available. And don't invite your really clever mates or the really stupid ones ... both types ask too many questions and waste time.

medical school   **SURVIVAL GUIDE**

hitting the books

We all know there are good books and bad books for last minute exam cramming. You'll find all the bad ones still stacked in the library the week before the exam. Those sussed-up students will have checked out the 'must-have' books months ago. They'll have had 'Borrow books for path exam' marked in their diary in bright red letters since they were in nappies.

Sure, 'hangin' out in the library aisles does nothing for the cool image you've spent the last three years creating, but this time you've got to bite your studded tongue, pull that 'hoodie' down so no-one will recognize you and face that complicated book indexing system.

A good way to know it's time for the exam book borrowing expedition is when the geeky kids start their foraging runs backwards and forward to the library. Get in, borrow, reserve or hide the books you want. Then get out. If you can't work out which ones are best ask someone or simply base your decision on which copies have the most coffee stains and teeth marks. Another good option is to check the sales ranking on the *Amazon.com* medical sales list online.

And don't discount public libraries either. If the book you want is all checked out at uni give your local public library a call (find the number at the website below). They might have it or be able to get it in a few days. You're likely to get a much longer loan period too.
www.lic.gov.uk

OSCE exams are like kidney stones – excruciating painful at the time but once you've passed them you no longer see what the big deal was. You'll also realise that despite the failings of the education system OSCEs are a really good way of testing your communication skills and, providing you haven't lost the power of speech, making sure even the dumbest students pass.

With people fainting, running out crying, and screaming at the uncooperative psyche patients, OSCE exams are madder than a West Ham footy match – and often much louder. With the stations crammed so close it can be difficult to hear yourself speak.

But a resourceful medical student can use this to their advantage. Seek out a highly skilled OSCE taker who's got a voice similar to a loudhailer. Stick to him like glue as you enter the OSCE room. Now you've got to be quick. Work out which direction you'll move round the room and get to the station behind your 'expert'.

Now it's time to put the plan into action. At rest stations you'll normally be able to read the question for the station ahead. Work through it yourself listening to your 'expert' next door remembering all the bits you would have left out. At regular stations you'll be testing your 'multi-tasking' skills to the limit. Always be careful not to be distracted from your current station.

Listening out for extra points in OSCE exams is a skill you'll develop during your years at medical school. We all just hope that the medical schools don't finally get organised enough to move OSCE exams to bigger rooms where you can't hear the answers.

Q: Negatively-marked MCQ exams are dreaded the most by medical students.
A: True.

Q: They assess medical knowledge only and not exam technique.
A: False.

Q: If you don't know an answer you should leave it blank.
A: Don't know?? Well read on ...

One of the biggest mistakes students make is leaving too many questions blank, says **Mark Healy** a student exam adviser. "It's too easy to be cautious especially when it comes to important exams," he says. "People who are prepared to take greater risks often get better marks without having greater knowledge."

If you've turned up for most lectures and done a bit of revision it's often worth a guess, proposes Healy. "You've got a higher chance of getting the question right than wrong, assuming you've done your homework. An occasional wrong answer should easily be cancelled out by the extra ones you've got correct."

It's also worth taking a look at your answering style, he suggests. "Do a practice MCQ paper answering all the questions but also mark how confident you are of the answer. Then when you mark it take a close look at how your correct answers correlate to your confidence level."

"You'll often find that you got questions right even when you were less confident," he says. "Bear this is mind when you come to your next MCQ paper and you'll pick up more marks."

As a medical student you're not expected to know the histological risk classification for cervical metaplasia. You are, however, expected to perform in a 'professional and competent manner with regard to the patient'. This is what the OSCE examines and you'll get most of your marks for just doing this. Here's some key points.

Check the name
"Mrs. Smith?" For results or serious topics also check the patient's date of birth/address. "Can I just confirm that your date of birth is February 23rd 1945??"

Good introduction
"Hello, my name is John Smith, one of the GPs attached to this practice. I've been asked to come and speak to you about the results of your cervical smear that was taken last week. Are you happy for me to discuss this with you now??"

Making the patient feel at ease
"Are you comfortable? If you want me to stop at any time just let me know and we can end it there." "Would you like to have anyone present with you?"

Beg for help to get those points
"Is there anything else that you'd like to mention, or anything that I have forgotten to ask you??" (ie. please help me!?!)

Any questions?
"Do you have any questions that you'd like to ask me?" ... and if they ask anything complicated – "I'm only a medical student/junior doctor/monkey so I don't really feel I can give you a well-informed answer. I'll ask the consultant if he can discuss it with you as he would be able to give you a much better answer."

Follow-up
"I'll ask the nurse to provide you with an information leaflet which you can take away and read. If you have any further questions please do not hesitate to ask us here at the surgery or make another appointment if necessary."

And by this stage you'll be pretty close to passing that station … even if you did think a cervical smear is used to investigate neck stiffness!!

The net can be an essential source of learning information – and not just the anatomy you learn on those porn sites. From online tutorials and interactive question sets to videos of examinations and theatre ops it definitely beats having your head stuck in traditional textbooks. Here's some useful sites.

anatomy

Cyberanatomy Tutorials • • •
Developed by the University of Newcastle and written by students it's a visual guide to most parts of the human body. There's also online video and lecture notes.
www.anatome.ncl.ac.uk/tutorials
Henry Gray – Anatomy of the Human Body • • •
Henry Gray was the ultimate anatomist. His book 'Gray's Anatomy' is still a bestseller. You'll find the entire anatomy textbook here – text, diagrams everything!!
www.bartleby.com/107
LUMEN Structure of the Human Body • •
Although it's got lots of tutorials and fancy diagrams the main reason to visit this site is to test yourself using their online quizzes – great for finding out how much you really know.
www.meddean.luc.edu/lumen/MedEd/GrossAnatomy

biochemistry

The Medical Biochemistry Page • • •
Medical biochemistry is one of the most torturous subjects you'll have to deal with during the course. We'd hoped to find some miracle site that could explain it in a language we could understand but failed. This is as close as we got. Check out the PowerPoint presentations.
www.dentistry.leeds.ac.uk/biochem/thcme/home.html

cardiology

Cardiology Site • • •
Very professional site which claims to offer the equivalent of 'classroom lectures and demonstrations with the use of the latest web-based technology' – and it does a pretty good job of it. Loads of 3D animations, videos and quizzes to get your heart pumping.
www.cardiologysite.com
ECGs by Example • • •
Until someone is clever enough to invent an ECG machine that prints out the abnormalities in words (it can't be that difficult, can it?) we're going to have to struggle to understand all those squiggles. This is the first of two ECG sites we'd recommend. This one lists the pathology and lets you look at the ECG.

medical school   SURVIVAL GUIDE

www.ecglibrary.com/ecghome.html

ECG Encyclopedia • • •

The second site presents you with a choice of 25 case studies. You then try and work out the abnormality, fail miserably, then look up the comprehensive answers. These are explained in a language which even the most ECG-inept student could understand.

sprojects.mmi.mcgill.ca/heart/molsonp-cb/project/biggie.htm

Cardiac Examination • • •

Seventeen minute video explaining how to examine the cardiovascular system (medical student level).

www.med-ed.virginia.edu/courses/pom1/videos/cardiac.cfm

Heart Sounds Tutorial • • • •

This is one great site. Very professional and packed with great graphics and functions. It's the perfect way to finally understand what's making all those noises in the patient's chest and what it should sound like when things go wrong.

www.blaufuss.org/tutorial

clinical examination

A Practical Guide to Clinical Examination • • • • •

Forget every other clinical examination site out there. You just need this one. It's a comprehensive guide to all systems with text, anatomical links, pictures and video. Also includes sections on presentations and 'putting it all together'. Totally invaluable.

medicine.ucsd.edu/clinicalmed/introduction.htm

Screening Physical Exam • • • •

An even more comprehensive examination guide than the one above but a little more complicated. Split into frames it guides you through the exam step-by-step. There's also lots of pictures of the clinical signs that you should be looking for.

www.meddean.luc.edu/lumen/MedEd/medicine/pulmonar/pd/contents.htm

Catalog of Clinical Images • • • •

Medical students get very good at examining healthy people. The problem comes when we actually get someone with physical abnormalities. This site has hundreds of images of the signs we should be able to spot when a patient presents with a pathology.

medicine.ucsd.edu/clinicalimg/browse.html

Breast Examination • • •

This superb video explaining how to examine the breast is designed for nurses but don't let that put you off. It's a well presented resource on a skill which is often difficult to practice in the clinical environment.

www.son.washington.edu/courses/aut03/nclin500/demos/breast-exam.ram

dermatology

DermAtlas • • •

Want to know what that little red lump on your right cheek is? Well, there's bound to be a picture of it here. This site contains over 5000 images – and not a single holiday

snap in sight!!
www.dermatlas.org
eMedicine •• ••
The eMedicine site is great for most medical subjects but for dermatology it beats any textbook hands down. It's got everything from differential diagnoses to treatment.
www.emedicine.com/derm/contents

gastroenterology

Abdominal Examination •••
Nine minute video explaining how to examine the abdomen (med student level).
www.med-ed.virginia.edu/courses/pom1/videos/abdomen.cfm

general medicine

eMedicine •• •••
Almost perfect. This has to be the world's best medical site. Every condition nicely categorised into signs, symptoms, differentials and treatment. All with pictures and diagrams. Amazing.
www.emedicine.com/med/
The Merck Manual ••
Funded by the pharmaceutical company Merck this series of 'non-profit' manuals are a huge comprehensive textbook. Great for looking up all those weird conditions.
www.merck.com/mrkshared/mmanual/sections.jsp
MedicalMnemonics •• ••
This site has hundreds of simple ways to remember those complicated lists of conditions. So next time you find yourself struggling to learn the ten symptoms of hyperadrenalism surf to this site to avoid the brain strain.
www.medicalmnemonics.com

genetics

Genetics Home Reference •••
Again, genetics is another subject likely to give you sleepless nights. This site from the US National Library of Medicine covers the simple stuff and complicated stuff well, but seems to have missed out the bit in the middle.
ghr.nlm.nihgov

histology

Histology Web Labs •• •
Nice collection of online PowerPoint slides that explain what you can see both histologically and from a clinical perspective. Great if you've missed any of those

medical school

histology tutorials
astro.temple.edu/ sodicm/labs

microbiology

Microbiology and Immunology Online • •
It's not exactly the most simply microbiology site, and you'll find that much of the text goes right over your head but don't let that put you off. The fantastic pictures, links and sheer amount of information should still make this your first microbiology stop.
www.med.sc.edu:85/book/welcome.htm

neurology

Neurologic - An Anatomical Approach to the Neurological Exam • • •
A site which closely combines neuroanatomy with the clinical exam giving you the chance to understand why you're actually doing certain tests. Great videos accompany the text.
medstat.med.utah.edu/neurologicalexam/
Neurological Examination • • •
Twelve minute video explaining how to examine the neurological system (med student level).
www.med-ed.virginia.edu/courses/pom1/videos/neuro.cfm

obstetrics and gynaecology

Human Reproduction • • • • •
Pitched perfectly at med student level this site has tutorials and lecture notes for all the main subjects. It focuses more on the obstetrics topics but that's not a bad thing as they're the trickier ones. There's an array of tests and slides to look at too.
medstat.med.utah.edu/kw/human_reprod/

orthopaedics

Electronic Orthopaedic Textbook • •
Not particularly the best organised site – it's essentially just a textbook dumped onto the net. But it's a very good textbook and this easily makes up for the difficult navigation. It's written especially for med students and junior doctors.
www.worldortho.com/database/etext/index.html
Shoulder Examination • • •
Four minute video explaining how to perform a shoulder examination (medical student level).
www.med-ed.virginia.edu/courses/pom1/videos/shoulder.cfm

SURVIVAL
GUIDE   *medical school*

Hip, Knee and Ankle Examination • • •
Twelve minute video explaining how to perform a examination of the leg and foot
(medical student level).
www.med-ed.virginia.edu/courses/pom1/videos/lowextrem.cfm

paediatrics

Case Based Paediatrics • • • •
Learn by case examples covering all subjects including neonatology and adolescent
medicine. All cases come with worked answers and lecture style notes. Each subject
also has MCQ style questions.
www.hawaii.edu/medicine/pediatrics/pedtext/pedtext.html
The New Children's Hospital Handbook • • •
Fantastic online paediatric textbook produced by a hospital in New South Wales,
Australia.
www.chw.edu.au/prof/handbook/toc.htm
picuBook • •
Not a great revision resource but an interesting site for those interested in paediatrics.
You'll find lots of video submissions from surgery and critical care cases. There's also
plenty of case studies and picture slides.
www.picubook.net

pathology

Interactive Pathology Laboratory • • •
Choose the condition (over 100 listed) and you'll be presented with the info on both the
clinical and histological pathology along with illustratory slides. Perfect for the path
required by the UK syllabus even though this is an American site.
www.iplab.net
The Internet Pathology Laboratory for Medical Education • • •
Nearly 2000 images along with text, tutorials, laboratory exercises and examination
items for self-assessment demonstrating gross and microscopic pathology.
www-medlib.med.utah.edu/WebPath/webpath.html
Lab Tests Online • • •
Designed for patients – so med students should be able to understand it too. You can
either choose the test or condition and get the background on why and how each
investigation takes place. Also includes a screening section useful for genetics and obs
and gynae related path.
www.labtestsonline.org
Path Notes - Cornell University • • •
Just great path notes. That's it.
edcenter.med.cornell.edu/CUMC_PathNotes/PathNotes.html
Virtual Autopsy • • •
Great for putting all the path you've learnt together in a fun format. You get to work

through a virtual autopsy and try to piece together a diagnosis.
www.le.ac.uk/pathology/teach/va/titlpag1.html

pharmacology

Internet Self Assessment in Pharmacology • •
Lots of pharmo tests to check how much you really know. The site is slightly
Americanised as expected but if you can cope with this it's an ideal assessment site.
You need to register first before you can use it. Registration is free but can take up to
three days to get a password.
www.horsetooth.com/ISAP/welcome.html

psychiatry

Internet Mental Health • •
A site full of clinical information for both patients and health professionals. As well as
educational content it's got the latest mental health news and regular articles.
www.mentalhealth.com

radiology

Radiology Chest X-Ray Review • • •
A step-by-step guide to the methodology for examining chest X-rays. It explains what
you should look for and how to spot any pathology that may be present.
rad.usuhs.mil/rad/chest_review/index.html
RadAnatomy • • •
As a medical student you're occasionally asked to present X-rays which is a pretty
scary task. In most cases you'll have trouble just working out which part of the body is
shown on the film. Try this X-ray anatomy tutor if you want to look slick.
classes.kumc.edu/som/radanatomy

respiratory

The RALE Respository • •
Patients can make all kinds of weird noises when they breath. This site helps you
understand the difference between crackles and croup. Complete with recordings of
lung sounds and respirograms.
www.rale.ca
Chest Examination • • •
Ten minute video explaining how to perform a chest examination (med student level).
www.med-ed.virginia.edu/courses/pom1/videos/chest.cfm

sexual health

Sexual Health History • • •
Two videos. The first is a three minute section on how to take a basic sexual history. The second is a seven minute section on sexual health issues related to history taking.
www.med-ed.virginia.edu/courses/pom1/videos/basic-sexual-hist.cfm
www.med-ed.virginia.edu/courses/pom1/videos/focused-sexual-hist.cfm

statistics

The Little Handbook of Statistical Practice • • • •
Why p=0.05? Who was 'student'? Finally, want to be able to understand that jumble of numbers that meant nothing before? Trust us, this site is statistically significant and our randomised trial showed students agree.
www.statisticalpractice.com

surgery

Learnsurgery.com • • • • •
A fantastic surgery site – and a British one at that!! Aimed perfectly at the level of med students it covers all the major topics through a series of twenty real-life case studies. Surgery quizzes help test your knowledge.
www.learnsurgery.com

Surgical-tutor.org.uk • • • •
Another great British site. Packed with notes, mcqs and slide libraries. It's great for medical students and even better for membership exams – so keep it bookmarked.
www.surgical-tutor.org.uk

stressed out?

It's hardly surprising. Messy housemates, end-of-firm exams, breaking up with your boyfriend, missing home cooking. It doesn't even have to be something big. Maybe you've lost your wallet, or the train is late again.

Sabina Dosani, specialist registrar in psychiatry, offers some advice on how to cope with the stresses and strains of medical school.

At low levels, increases in stress lead to improved performance. Low level stress is essential for survival as a medical student, helping you learn and produce work to high standards. But, when peak performance is reached, further stress has catastrophic results. Typically, tiredness is the first sign. Exhaustion and mental health problems follow if stress continues unchecked.

getting on top of work

Stress causes a surge of noradrenaline in the synaptic cleft, inducing a feeling of elation. It is also why so many of us put off work until the last minute, chasing the "deadline high". Its flipside is that when unexpected things happen, like the computer crashing or printer cartridges running out at midnight, or a catastrophic crisis occurs, stress levels soar.

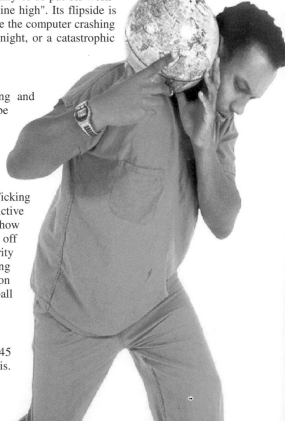

plan ahead

Set aside time each week for planning and organising work. Sunday evenings can be good for this, although traditionally this time is used to complete work due in on Monday morning.

get organised

Consider using a daily 'to do' list. Ticking things as you do them is strangely addictive and gives you a buzz as you realise how much you've achieved. Everyone puts off things they don't like. Identify high priority tasks. Do these first and stop them piling up. Don't forget to include fun stuff on your list. A dance class, film or football training.

time tips

Concentration spans rarely exceed 45 minutes. You need a break after this.

Everybody has times when they feel sluggish. Are you an early bird, post-prandial procrastinator or night owl? Identify your least productive time. Use it for filing handouts or typing references into an essay, not for learning all the branches of the brachial plexus.

chunk it up

If you can't eat a big bar of chocolate in one go, you break it up into bits. Why not do the same with work? Writing 500 words of a 3000 word dissertation every night means you'll be finished by the weekend and not have to burn midnight oil on Sunday.

no thanks

While getting involved in extracurricular activities is generally a good thing, taking on more commitments than you can cope with isn't. You may aspire to captain the rugby team, direct the Christmas panto and edit the student mag but can you muster the energy for everything? Learn to say no.

a friend in need

Maybe your friend is in trouble? You might not know what to say or do. If someone is stressed and upset, how should friends react?

Do: Listen and let them know you want to help.
         Help them find professional advice if you are out of your depth.
Don't: Tell your friend what to do. Your best solution might not work for them.
         Break confidentiality unless you are worried about your friend's safety.

---

bad (but common ways to deal with stress)

alcohol
At first, alcohol makes you feel relaxed. For most medical students social drinking doesn't become a problem. But if you regularly use alcohol to solve problems, to sleep or relax you're heading for trouble.

Practice safe drinking – at most 3-4 units. If you have a few alcohol free days each week dependence is a lot less likely.

caffeine
Caffeine raises levels of adrenaline and noradrenaline making feelings of stress worse. A mug of tea contains the same amount of caffeine as a cup of instant coffee.

smoking
So smoking makes you feel relaxed? Try this. Take your pulse before and after a cigarette. Enough said.

---

better ways to cope with stress

exercise
Any sustained regular exercise triggers a chemical reaction in the body producing hormones called endorphins. These endorphins produce a natural high, which is why you feel good after strenuous physical activity. It doesn't necessarily mean the gym. Dancing all night at a club produces endorphins too.

relax
Find a way to relax and practice it often. It might be soaking in a candle-lit bath with your favourite music in the background followed by a massage. Remember how you used to unwind? Just because you are a medical student doesn't mean you have to put away your paintbrushes or flute.

talking
If you feel stressed it is likely that you are not alone. Find someone to grumble with for half an hour. You will probably feel better. If you are sliding down the slippery stress slope tell a friend. They can help you find appropriate help and give you the courage to speak to your tutor before you start to under-perform big time. Struggling on and failing exams will make you feel worse.

counselling
Consider paying a visit to your student counselling service. Counsellors are trained to help you find solutions to problems.

what to expect
Your first 'session' will be an assessment. You will usually be seen in a comfortable private room, without interruptions for about 50 minutes. You will have a chance to describe how you feel. The counsellor will try to understand more about you and how best to help you. Sometimes they suggest other agencies more suited to your needs. If you both agree counselling could help you will be offered a course of 'sessions'. Ten is typical.

local resources
Your tutor, student welfare officer, GP or student health centre, university chaplaincy.

national resources
- BMA Counselling Service - 08459 200169 - a confidential telephone counselling service for BMA members (including medical student members and their families).
- National Drugs Helpline - 0800 776600 - Helpline offering information, counselling and advice about drug misuse. Refers callers to local agencies.

medical
school

SURVIVAL
GUIDE

intercalated
degrees

hotting up

Should I or shouldn't I?? Do I want to spend a year longer at university?? Will I be able to get the job I want without one?? Tumour biology, medical journalism … or maybe ethics and law??

Ahhhh!! If you're finding that choosing an intercalated degree should be a course in itself, check out our guide below.

two degrees

Not content with putting us through five years of a medical degree the universities are now expecting us to take on an extra BSc or BA. It's not something that's often explained before you start medical school but the majority of us will actually spend six years before we qualify and leave with two degrees.

Ultimately you do get the choice of whether to do an intercalated degree or not. The problem is that as it's now the norm you're at a serious disadvantage if you don't. It's a difficult decision to make. We've listed some of the key advantages and disadvantages below to help you make up your mind.

advantages

It's a break from medicine
After a few years of vomiting patients and day-after-day of microbiology lectures a break from the medical course might seem quite appealing.
Stay with your mates
All your friends may be doing an intercalated degree meaning you would be left venturing on ahead with the medical course alone.
Get interested
Surprisingly, you might actually find one of the courses on offer really appealing. It might even lead you to pursue a career in neuropsychology you'd never considered.
Be more competitive
If you intend to pursue a competitive specialty, or one of the more sought after house

jobs it might be necessary. When consultants come to sorting through a pile of similar applicants they look for some way to discard CVs from the 'to interview' pile. Sorting them into 'have BSc' and 'have not' is a common practice – so beware.

Cramming that CV

Intercalated degrees are a chance to obtain those sought after presentations and publications to help bolster your CV.

Stay a student

You're going to get stuck doing medicine for the rest of your life once you qualify, so take your time getting there. Life as a student is really quite good!!

Take a break

Most intercalated degrees have less lectures, more days off and longer holidays.

disadvantages

Delaying the inevitable

It's one more year as a student – and one extra year till you qualify.

Counting the cost

Stumping up the cost of fees (if your LEA won't) along with your living expenses may make you feel like you don't have the choice anyway. Don't rule it out though, there's plenty of organizations offering bursaries for intercalated degrees. You'll also have a longer summer to get a part time job.

Returning to medicine

If you do an intercalated degree you'll still have to come back and finish the medical course. Returning to three more years can be difficult.

Motivational misery

There's often lots of self-study which can prove difficult if you're not easily motivated.

Tough enough

The idea of extra holidays and a proper summer break may sound appealing but it's not always this easy in reality. There are students who virtually live in their labs and some courses have extremely tough exams and project components.

london

barts and london
BMedSci Community Health Sciences
BMedSci Molecular Medicine
BMedSci Molecular Therapeutics
Clinical Materials
Experimental Pathology
Human Bioscience
Biomedical Engineering
Neuroscience
Oral Biology

Tel - 0207 3777747
www.mds.qmul.ac.uk/intercalated

gkt
Anatomy, Cell & Human Biology
Aerospace Physiology
Biochemistry
Biology
Biomaterials
Biomolecular Science
Clinical Healthcare, Ethics and Law
Developmental Neurobiology
Endocrinology
Human Genetics
Immunology
Infectious Diseases & Immunobiology
Maternal & Fetal Medicine
Microbiology
Modern Language Centre
Molecular Aspects of the Diseases
  of Aging
Neuroscience
Nutrition
Oral Biology
Pharmacology
Philosophy

Physiology
Psychology
Radiological Sciences

Tel - 0207 848 6400
www.kcl.ac.uk/biomedical

imperial
Endocrinology
Haematology
Management and Basic Medical
  Sciences
Neuroscience
Imaging
Immunobiology
Physiology

Tel - 0207 594 9811

st. georges
Basic Medical Science
No external applicants
Tel - 0208 672 9944

Medical Genetics
External applicants accepted
Tel - 0208 7250229
acrosby@sghms.ac.uk

ucl
Anatomy and Developmental Biology
Biochemistry and Molecular Biology
History of Medicine
Human Genetics
Immunology and Cell Pathology
Infection
International Health

Medical Anthropology
Medical Humanities
Medical Physics
Molecular Medicine
Neuroscience
Orthopaedic Science
Pharmacology
Physiology
Pharmacology and Physiology
Primary Health Care
Psychology
Speech Science and Communication
Tumour Biology

Tel - 0207 679 5477

westminster
Medical Journalism BA

Tel - 0207 9115903
harrow-admissions@wmin.ac.uk
www.geocities.com/coursesite

rest of uk

aberdeen
Medical Sciences

Open to internal applicants
Tel - 01224 553014

belfast
Anatomy
Biochemistry
Physiology
Molecular Biology
Microbiology
Pathology

Pharmacology
Cardiovascular Science

www.qub.ac.uk/cm/pat/ibsc
b.mcdermott@qub.ac.uk
Tel - 02890 2772242

birmingham
BMedSci Behavioural Science
BMedSci Public Health
BMedSci Occupational Health
BMedSci Ethics & Law
BMedSci History of Medicine

Open to external applicants
Also BSc courses. Internal applicants
should check course info.
Tel - 0121 4143510
medweb.bham.ac.uk/bmedsci/bmshome.
html

bristol
Anatomical Science
Human Musculoskeletal Science
Biochemistry
Bioethics
Neuroscience
Cancer Biology
Cancer Biology & Immunology
Immunology
Medical Microbiology
Pathology & Microbiology
Virology & Immunology
Pharmacology
Physiological Sciences

Tel - 0117 9289957

cambridge

No intercalated degrees

dundee
Anatomy
Biochemistry
Applied Orthopaedic Technology
Cellular and Molecular Basis of Disease
Forensic Medicine
Medical Psychology
Pharmacology
Pharmacology & Neuroscience
Physiology

Tel - 01382 632763
facmd@dundee.ac.uk

edinburgh
Biochemistry
Epidemiology
Genetics
Immunology
Microbiology & Infection
Molecular Biology
Neuroscience
Experimental Pathology
Pharmacology
Pharmacology with Industrial
  Experience
Physiology
Psychology
Developmental Biology
Medical Biology
Reproductive Biology
Sports Science Medicine
Zoology

Tel - 0131 6503190
www.med.ed.ac.uk/studying/honschl.
htm

glasgow
Anatomical Sciences
Biochemistry
Clinical Medicine
Genetics
Immunity in Health and Disease
Microbiology
Molecular and Cellular Biology
Parasitology
Pharmacology
Physiology
Psychological Medicine

Tel - 0141 3304424

leeds
Biochemistry
Clinical Sciences
Genetics
Health Care Ethics
History of Medicine
International Health
Microbiology
Neuroscience
Pharmacology
Physiology
Psychology
Sports Science
Zoology

Tel - 0113 2334364
www.leeds.ac.uk/medicine/learning/bsc.
htm

leicester/warwick
Two options:
1) BSc with various modules
2) 9 month research program

Internal students only

Tel - 0116 252 2969

liverpool
Anatomy and Human Biology
Biochemisty
Genetics
Microbiology
Molecular Biology
Pharmacology
Physiology
Tropical Disease Biology

Tel - 0151 7064268
www.liv.ac.uk/facmed/intercalbookmas.
htm

manchester
Anatomical Science
Biochemistry
Biomedical Science
Cell Biology
Health Care Ethics and Law
History of Medicine
Medical Biochemistry
Neuroscience
Pathology
Pharmacology
Pharmacology and Physiology
Physiology
Masters in Population Health Evidence
Psychology

Tel - 0161 2757201
ug.medicine.man.ac.uk/ug_current/doc/
handbooks2004/ihandbook2004_2005.
pdf

newcastle
Biochemistry
Biochemistry with Biotechnology

Biochemistry with Immunology
Biomedical Sciences Genetics
Human Genetics
Medical Microbiology
Medical Microbiology and Immunology
Molecular Biology
Pharmacology
Physiological Sciences

Tel - 0207 5949813

nottingham
BMedSci (part of med degree)
No external course

Tel - 0115 9249924
kate.squires@nottingham.ac.uk

oxford
No intercalated courses
Oxford students can intercalate elsewhere between pre-clinical and clinical
years

Tel - 01865 221681

sheffield
BMedSci - advertised internally

Internal students only
Tel - 0114 2712932

southampton
Biomedical Science
Sociology
Psychology
Courses last two years, overlaps with
clinical year.

Tel - 023 80594338
bmadmissions@soton.ac.uk

wales
Pharmacology
Physiology
Biochemistry
Anatomical Science
Cognitive Neuroscience
Exercise Science

Tel - 029 20742063

table key (opp)

Integrated - These medical schools now include an intercalated degree as part of a 6-year course.

All allowed - Any student who wishes to take an intercalated degree course is allowed in all but exceptional cases, although this may have to be at an alternative university/course.

Restrictions - Limits are placed on the number of students who can take an intercalated course.

Not allowed - No students are permitted to take an intercalated course at their host university or elsewhere.

Notes
1. Cambridge only offers the pre-clinical medical course.
2. Nottingham students complete the BMedSci as part of their 5-year degree course. They are not permitted to take a course elsewhere.

	integrated	all allowed	restrictions	no one allowed
Barts & London			•	
GKT		•		
Imperial	•			
St. Georges			•	
UCL	•			
Aberdeen			•	
Belfast (Queens)			•	
Birmingham			•	
Bristol			•	
Cambridge[1]				•
Dundee		•		
Edinburgh			•	
Glasgow			•	
Leeds		•		
Leicester		•		
Liverpool		•		
Manchester			•	
Newcastle			•	
Nottingham[2]				•
Oxford			•	
Sheffield		•		
Southampton			•	
Wales			•	

SURVIVAL GUIDE *medical school*

With over 170 intercalated courses on offer finding one that suits you can be a difficult search. There's not just the subject to pick but which university to attend as course programs vary a great deal depending on the location.

There's no better way to find out about a course than to ask previous intercalaters. We've included reviews of some of the more unusual courses below. You can find many more at the intercalated section of the traumaroom.com website.

medical journalism - westminster

what's it about?
It may be called 'medical' journalism but it's only very loosely related to medicine. The course teaches you more about journalism as a profession and only touches on medicine as an interesting topic for a journalist to write about.

who'd want to do it?
Someone who wants a complete break from medicine or is on the lookout for a change of career.

entry requirements?
Applicants must have completed two years of a health related degree, then shortlisted candidates are asked to attend an interview. The prospectus threatens you with an English language exam too but that doesn't always happen.

course content
Modules are in journalism theory, law and politics as well as more creative teaching on medical news and feature writing. Students learn shorthand, become competent with digital cameras and a range of computer software such as Dreamweaver,

QuarkXpress and Photoshop. There is also the opportunity to complete a three week work attachment with a publication of your choice.

how is it assessed?
Mostly on coursework completed throughout the year consisting of essays and group work – putting together an online newspaper and magazine. There are also exams in shorthand, theory and law, and there is an assessed 'reporting week' where all of the acquired skills are put to the test!!

was it well run?
The course has been running a few years now and, apart from room shortages at times, ran quite smoothly in close conjunction with the more established postgraduate diploma in journalism. There are regular meetings between students and staff to iron out any problems.

the best points
1 Acquiring journalistic skills encase medicine goes pear shaped.
2 A year in London.

3 Seeing medicine from a journalist's point of view.

the worst points
1 More exams.
2 Mastering shorthand.
3 Seeing medicine from a journalist's point of view.

in conclusion
In the five years of medicine would you be actively encouraged to make your own website? Dig up scandalous stories from the depths of the student union? Cavort around campus dressed as a giant mouse? Probably not, but things like this were commonplace during a year of medical journalism. It was a great experience and we learnt some highly useful skills and had a laugh along the way.
Ellen Welch

history of medicine - manchester

what's it about?

The history of medicine course provides an excellent opportunity to explore artistic terrain that is unlikely to be available to many on the standard medical degree. Covering Greek medicine to the AIDS crisis, the course has the potential to interest and be of use to almost anyone involved in medicine.

who'd want to do it?

It would be most useful to those who want to stretch their capabilities, learn more about the truth behind medicine and develop skills in analysis, argument and (of course!) essay writing.

entry requirements?

You must have completed 2 years of the undergraduate course.

course content

Modules available at CHSTM include 'medicine before 1800', literature and medicine, ethical and political aspects of medicine in the 19th century, 20th century medicine, research skills, and many more.

Certain modules are core, others optional. In the second semester a dissertation on the subject of your choice must be completed.

how is it assessed?

Each module is assessed by exam and essay in equal proportion. That means three essays and three exams in the first semester, four essays and four exams in the second semester, and a dissertation.

was it well run?

It was a well run course with excellent support provided, clear guidelines and good feedback. No technical hitches occurred that I can remember, and although most of the staff have only trained in history they generally understand that medical students may find the transition to arts difficult.

the best points

1 Fascinating subject.

2 Broadens horizons.

3 Good tutor support.

the worst points

1 It's a tough year and you have to be prepared to

persevere.

2 Making the transition from science to arts.

3 Writing essays.

in conclusion

The history of medicine course at CHSTM is excellent and well worth the challenge. Apart from academic life, being in the university of Manchester provided me with a different view of life from a medical school in London where I am training. I would strongly urge people from outside Manchester to consider doing the course. I have benefited greatly from the year: gaining confidence in understanding and communicating historical ideas, participating in a lively, cosmopolitan city, and broadening my horizons beyond the sphere of undergraduate medicine.

Laura Caley

tumour biology - ucl

what's it about?

Tumour biology is a really interesting topic which is highly relevant whatever career path you choose whether it's kids, care of the elderly, obs and gynae or GP. It covers a range of related topics

beginning with the molecular basis of cancer, then going onto metastasis, carcinogens and ending with an unit into treatment.

who'd want to do it?

Someone who's interested in both the scientific and clinical

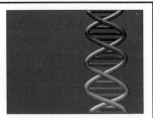

side of cancer and doesn't mind a fair bit of reading and essay writing!!

entry requirements?
The requirements were to have passed all my pre-clinical exams. You may be called for an interview.

course content
There are five core modules: cancer research, cell biology of neoplasia, metastasis and tumour invasion, and cancer and the environment. Most people also do an extra module which covers the treatment of cancer. There is a six week lab-based research project, which gives the opportunity to study a cancer of interest in more detail.

how is it assessed?
Each unit was assessed on the basis of a presentation and an essay assignment. The majority of marks for each unit was an exam at the end. The project at the end counted for 2/7 of the final exam.

was it well run?
The course was very well structured. We received very comprehensive hand-outs and reading lists for each lecture, which directed our learning and meant having to write less notes!! Most people really enjoyed their research projects and the tutors were generally keen to help.

the best points
1 Well structured and helpful staff.

2 Clinically relevant.

3 Opportunity to do up-to-date research into a cancer of interest.

the worst points
1 Coping with essay writing again.

2 Having to plough through journals.

3 Spending 6 weeks in a lab (which I enjoyed!!) may not be for everyone.

in conclusion
An absolutely fab year. Great opportunity to learn about cancers, meet new people and to experience life at another college. The project, although being lots of fun, is not for the faint-hearted!! It involved early starts and long evenings in the lab, while busily trying to write the whole thing up. If you're interested in cancers, and want to learn more from people at the forefront of research then this is the BSc for you.

Deboshree Basu-Choudhuri

---

psychology - edinburgh

what's it about?
It's an observational and experimental science concerned with the understanding and explanation of behaviour and experience.

who'd want to do it?
Someone who would like to expand their scientific learning outside of the lab or ward, and who doesn't mind reading ... a lot.

entry requirements?
You must have completed your first two years of medicine and have a better than average position in the year.

course content
Psychology is normally a four-year course. As intercalated medics we had to complete 3 ten week third year courses (e. g. perception, cognition, biological, social psychology) as well as 6 five week fourth year courses (choose from a wide range such as reading and dyslexia, appetite and eating, parapsychology, psychological therapies) over two terms of ten weeks. We also had to carry out a project (expected to take at least 100 hours) and write it up as a 11,500 word dissertation. I studied the personality of chimpanzees in Edinburgh zoo (!).

how is it assessed?

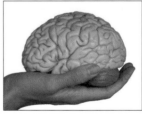

Two exams on the third year subjects, four on the fourth year subject and the dissertation.

was it well run?
It's an established course but it was a bit confusing at the start as we weren't really told when and where we were supposed to be.

the best points
1 You get to study topics that you will never cover in

medicine, most of which are interesting.

2 Only 5-9 hrs of lectures/ tutorials a week and you can seriously claim that going to the zoo is work.

3 It's not medicine.

the worst points

1 Reading until your eyes bleed.

2 Going straight into fourth year and be expected to contribute as much at tutorials as people who have had a three-year headstart.

3 It's not medicine.

in conclusion

I'm glad that I did it but I wouldn't want to do it again. While most of the stuff we covered was interesting, there was so much reading to do that it made everything dull. Having said that, it was fantastic to do something so different for a year, even if we did have to mix with social scientists!!

David Armstrong

physiology - imperial

what's it about?

This course is taught by preclinical teachers and the relevance to clinical medicine is highlighted throughout the course. The course allows you to choose two of four modules to study from Renal, Endocrinology, Neuromuscular and Vascular Physiology.

who'd want to do it?

This course is very practical with little theoretical/formal lectures (20!). Someone who has no clue at all about reading medical literature will be taught and there is a high probability you will get at least one publication.

entry requirements?

You must have completed the first two years of medical school.

course content

You study two modules in the first term. I studied renal and endocrinology. The second and third terms were spent carrying out a lab based project in any physiological field you wish.

how was it assessed?

Each of the 2 modules was a

1/3 of the degree. Half of a module was in course assessment (1 essay/1 mini project/project presentation) the other half was a 3 hour written exam on 10 lectures requiring you to learn about 3 papers for each lecture. The last 1/3 of the course was the research project and 10,000 write up and external viva.

was it well run?

The teachers are some of the best in the world and they have run this course for many years. There were always past students to confide in and past papers available to work out exam patterns.

the best points

1 You'll be able to look back to your degree to help you with clinical topics.

2 There is lots of time set aside for research which you will inevitably have to do if you want a hospital job.

3 You'll have a lot of free time so you can really enjoy your year and a 5 month summer holiday!!

the worst points

1 You'll lots of free time so you can get quite bored of daytime TV.

2 Hate labs? Then it's not for you!

3 Only a few people have ever received 1sts, nearly everyone gets a 2:1.

in conclusion

Doing Physiology at Imperial college was an eye opener as I saw for the first time what it was like to be a proper student like my non-medical friends. Socially I have never had such an amazing year which included a three month trip to USA and Canada. I got a publication out of my project in the Journal of Physiology and this has encouraged me further to carry out more research but in a clinical setting which will undoubtedly enhance my hospital medicine job prospects.

Shiva Dindyal

molecular medicine - ucl

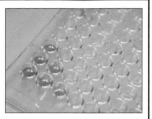

what's it about?
Molecular Medicine is a fascinating subject underpinning the basic medical sciences. This BSc covers the new developments in molecular and cellular biology and their applications to clinical medicine, while enabling hands on experience of the latest laboratory techniques.

who'd want to do it?
You should consider this if you liked biochemistry and are thinking about doing research at some point. Not a good choice for an easy year out of medicine.

entry requirements?
You must have passed the first 2 years of medicine. There are no interviews. The subject will feel a lot more relevant if you have done some clinical studies beforehand, but this isn't essential.

course content
There is one compulsory course unit in molecular biology and a choice of a literature review or 6-week research project. You can choose modules on the genetic basis of disease, the molecular aspects of Cardiovascular disease, molecular Oncology, Endocrinology and molecular advances in Reproductive Medicine.

how is it assessed?
75% of the marks for each module are from an end of year exam and the remaining 25% from in-course assessment. The lab project is assessed on the lab performance, seminars and write-up. The literature review is based solely on the written report.

was it well run?
The course is nicely structured with good teaching and comprehensive reading lists, but it does mean you are constantly working from the start of the year. Our lab project was scheduled to end a month before finals, which is pretty tight considering most projects run over, but the course is currently being modified so this may change.

the best points
1 The opportunity to design your very own research project.
2 The continuous assessment ensures that you don't leave all your revision until just before finals.
3 The small year group.

the worst points
1 There are one or two exams every term and it can feel like you are working all the time.
2 This BSc is based at the Royal Free, which can feel a bit isolating if you are used to being at a university that has subjects other than medicine.
3 The small year group.

in conclusion
I enjoyed Molecular Medicine, but it involved a lot of hard work. There are easier options. Lectures start at 9am every day and your social life suffers around each assessment (and there are many assessments!). This BSc provides a deeper understanding of clinical medicine, and creates a good grounding for future research work.

Marianna Thomas

medical school **SURVIVAL GUIDE**

medical
school

SURVIVAL
GUIDE

electives

get away

If you dare ask any doctor their best experience at medical school then you'd better be prepared for hours of mind-numbing stories from their medical elective – and if you're really unlucky they'll even whip out a photo album bigger than the entire *Encyclopedia Britannica.*

Your medical elective is guaranteed to be an amazing experience – and it'll soon be your eyes that light up when you get the chance to subject some unknowing medical student to stories of your time debriding ingrown toe-nails in the outer depths of Timbuktu.

Right now you're probably more scared than excited about your elective. You've just travelled 200 miles to medical school and that was traumatic enough. Hitch-hiking 3,000 miles into the deepest, darkest depths of the Amazon rainforest where people screw up their faces in confusion when you ask directions to the nearest *McDonalds* probably doesn't seem that appealing right now.

Well, it will. After you've endured the wrath of an ex-med student's elective epilogue and a similar dose of '*Wish You Were Here?*' you'll wish you were anywhere *but* here. It'll be all you think of for a while – perfect for daydreaming your way through all those neurology lectures.

On the downside however it's not quite as easy as booking a last minute package holiday off *Teletext*. There's a lot of planning to do. But don't worry, follow our guide below and we'll get you half way there – the rest is up to you.

so when do I get exported overseas?

Virtually all med schools have their elective periods towards the end of fourth year or during final year. Most have finally developed enough common sense to have final exams before you go meaning you no longer have to use half your baggage allowance for revision textbooks.

Some schools split the year into groups allowing them to go at different times. Use this

SURVIVAL GUIDE | *medical school*

to your advantage if you're going to the southern hemisphere and want to be there in summer. Tell the registry early and get them to put you in that group. You'll also find that some of the more specialised elective programs only take students during certain months.

how long can i be away for?

The average elective period allocated by medical schools is eight weeks. Most throw in a few weeks holiday afterwards so you can top-up your tan before returning back to tease your mates. These are a 'reward' for the two months of hard work that you have (in theory) completed.

If your curriculum includes special study modules there's a good chance you'll be able to attach these to your elective period. Four weeks cardiology is much more bearable when you can spend your lunch breaks on a sunny beach in the Caribbean rather than staring out through a rainy hospital canteen window in Britain.

where to go?

Whale watching off the coast of Australia?? Or trauma training in Tanzania?? ... choosing your destination is the toughest decision you'll have to make when planning your elective. You'll need to decide whether you're aiming for a pure holiday, some real medical experience or want to combine a bit of both.

Florida may be great for riding the rollercoasters at *Disneyworld* and checking out the babes on the beach but it's not going to give you the same life-defining experience as visiting a remote desert tribe in Africa with a medical outreach team.

Still don't have a clue where? Here's some useful feedback from students who've visited the most popular destinations.

south africa

Holiday Location   • • • •
Medical Experience   • • • • •
Total Cost   • • •

Picking a hospital in one of the townships or an outreach clinic means you'll get as much trauma as your stomach can handle ... often more!! You'll get hands on experience removing machetes from people's necks along with more mundane presentations. The effects of AIDS can be quite unsettling.

In South Africa you can go on safari and enjoy whale watching the same day. Cape Town is the city to visit and don't forget the great beaches – they rival any elsewhere.

medical school **SURVIVAL GUIDE**

india

Holiday Location • • • •
Medical Experience • • • •
Total Cost • • •

Quickly becoming one of the most popular elective destinations India has a lot to offer. Your medical experience whether you choose the mountainous north, desert-like West or one of the major cities is bound to be eventful. You'll see some rare diseases and see how medicine copes in a third-world state.

Knowing English is usually enough to get by and if you're on a tight budget it's simply unbeatable. Many students split their elective in two parts spending time in both the big city and in a rural environment.

usa

Holiday Location • • • •
Medical Experience • • • •
Total Cost • • • • •

If you thought that life was tough as a UK medical student then you're in for a shock. You'll be treated like US trainees working nights and thrown in at the deep end.

You might be surprised at how much clinical knowledge US students have but you'll notice they lack the science behind the diseases. It's not quite ER ... but this is a much closer comparison than Casualty!!

It can be expensive. Many US teaching hospitals levy a charge to spend your elective there. It can be as much as $1000 but normally includes accommodation. If you plan to work in the US and/or sit the USMLE exams an elective here can be really beneficial. Away from the hospital the US is a great place to have a holiday. It's such a vast country that there's plenty to do as long as you enjoy traveling and have enough time.

australia & new zealand

Holiday Location • • • • •
Medical Experience • •
Total Cost • • • • •

Probably the most popular elective destination ... and it's easy to see why!! It's English speaking, the weather's great and with attractions like diving in the Great Barrier Reef it seems unbeatable. On the downside your medical experience will be pretty poor. You'll find it much the same as the UK ... except most tutors will actively encourage you to bunk off and go and enjoy yourself!!

Sydney is a definite must to visit but if you choose to spend the elective part of your holiday away from the major cities and you'll get a much better medical experience.

caribbean

Holiday Location • • • •
Medical Experience • • •
Total Cost • • • • •

There's lots of options here from the excellent health care system of communist Cuba, to the trauma capital of the Caribbean, Jamaica. There's also the exclusive American-ised resorts of Bermuda and the British Virgin Islands.

You'll have plenty of opportunity for island hopping and for spending lunchtimes on the sun-drenched beaches working on that tan!!

Medical experience varies from island to island and you'll meet plenty of American students. You may even be attached to one of the American offshore medical schools.

south america

Holiday Location • • • • •
Medical Experience • • • •
Total Cost • • • •

The beaches of Copacabana, the Inca trail through the Andes, the Amazon rainforest and the culture and exuberance of South American culture have to make this one of the best destinations.

Medical care is still vastly underdeveloped so you can expect to be thrown in at the deep end. You have the option of working in the cities and 'favellas', with tribes in the jungle regions or even in the mountainous terrain of Peru and Bolivia. Wherever you go it will be unforgettable!!

Travel to and from South America can be expensive but once you're there it's as cheap as nacho chips!! Knowledge of Spanish or Portuguese is essential.

uk

Holiday Location •
Medical Experience • •
Total Cost •

Don't get too depressed if you can't afford to jet off to the sunshine. There's plenty on offer here in the great old British Isles. Specialist electives at Great Ormond Street Children's Hospital, or time with the Helicopter Emergency Medical Service in London can be amazing. Both can be particularly useful to enhance your career prospects if you fancy a job in this area.

Check out where other med students went and what they thought on the discussion boards at our elective site ...

www.
traumaroom
.com

medical school   **SURVIVAL GUIDE**

other options

Still not found the location for that perfect elective? Don't give up yet, there's plenty of options that don't fit the standard elective package. If you like to be different then here's some suggestions ...

NASA (Kennedy Space Center) - Very, very competitive. You need to apply a few years in advance and have enough 'special interests' to justify your selection. You'll get to spend time with the medical team supervising astronaut training and selection. There's also a chance to help with research into space and aviation. Placements usually only last a couple of weeks but can easily be attached to additional rotations in the US. *medic.ksc.nasa.gov/edu*

Royal Flying Doctor Service of Australia - Not too difficult to get onto – even at the last minute!! All reports from students have been great. You'll fly to remote communities in the outback to offer GP-type services and emergency aid. Most units are attached to a major hospital or clinic so you can experience the best of both worlds. *www.rfds.org.au*

Cruise Ships - Fantastic chance to visit some of the best and most exclusive countries in the world. Difficult to get the med school to understand that you're not just having a holiday, and to persuade the cruise company to accept you at a free/discounted fare. *www.cunard.co.uk*
www.pocruises.com

HM Prisons - If you've always wanted to experience life behind bars here's the easy way – without even having to commit a crime. Placements are available with experienced GPs in both Belmarsh (London) and Frankland (Durham) Prisons. Support is available for accommodation and they promise no bars on your windows. *www.hmprisonservice.gov.uk*

Amazon Health Team - If you don't mind bugs, snakes and swimming with piranhas this could be the elective for you. You'll journey deep into the rainforest with doctors visiting tribes offering medication and immunisations. Definitely an elective you'll never forget ... if you make it back in one piece!! *www.amazonafrica.org/Volunteer.html*

Himalayan Health Exchange - Looking for one BIG elective?? ... well you can't get bigger than this. This elective placement based in the shadow of Mount Everest is a well-structured program revolving around community and international health provision. It's designed with a mountain expedition in mind before or after the program – if you find that kind of thing appealing. *www.himalayanhealth.com/student.htm*

Now that you've decided a month in outer Mongolia is the elective for you, the next challenge is to find a placement that will take you on. To do this you'll need to contact a hospital or medical school in the destination you've chosen. The best way is to ask around to find someone who has been to the same region. If however you've chosen some far flung part of the world where no medical student has ever ventured before, then the next step is to get hooked up to the web.

MedicsTravel (www.medicstravel.co.uk) is an ideal starting point. It's got a list of countries along with contact details of the relevant medical institutions. You'll find the telephone numbers, addresses and websites of all the possible destinations. A print version is also available – *'Medics Guide to Work and Electives Around the World' (Mark Wilson; ISBN 0340760982).*

If you can't find an institution in your chosen destination try searching *Google*, or an equivalent search engine. If the hospital is lucky enough to have a website try to find the teaching coordinator or equivalent. If not, email the main hospital address and ask for the details of the person who deals with elective enquiries.

Email is definitely the best option for arranging electives. Writing letters is commonly suggested but it's painfully slow and unreliable. Don't be afraid to follow-up any correspondence by telephone as this is often the only way to get a response.

On the next page you can find a time-saving sample email which you can edit to your requirements.

Once you've been accepted ask for confirmation. Remember that your medical school will require some written documentation that you have been accepted on a program.

raising the cash

Travelling the world can be an expensive experience, but don't panic if your current budget only stretches to a weekend in Brighton. There are plenty of charities and trust funds willing to help pay for that plane ticket to paradise.

On the following pages you'll find a list of some on offer. Remember that they're not all going to be open to your plans but it's worth checking which might support you. Contact those that are appropriate and ask for an application form.

In return they may ask you to submit a report on your elective experience, or make a short presentation at one of their events. It may sound harsh but it's not a bad exchange for a round-the-world plane ticket.

```
┌─────────────────────────────────────────────────────────┐
│  ▢  elective email                                  ▨▨   │
├─────────────────────────────────────────────────────────┤
```

To: | *admin@outer-mongolia-district-hospital.org* |

From: | *joe.bloggs@dudleymedschool.ac.uk* |

Subject: | *Medical Student Electives at Outer Mongolia District Hospital* |

Dear Mrs. O'Vary,

My name is Joe Bloggs, a fifth year medical student at Dudley Medical School in England. As part of our training we are encouraged to complete an elective period overseas.

I was hoping that it may be possible to spend part of my elective at Outer Mongolia District Hospital. I have a particular interest in neurosurgery and it would be great if I could spend time in this specialty. Alternatively I would appreciate if you could let me know of any other placements that may be available.

The period I have been allocated for my elective is the 12th November 2004 to 3rd February 2005. Ideally I would like to spend approximately six weeks during this period at Outer Mongolia District Hospital if this would be possible.

I am happy to forward a copy of my CV and references to you.

Hopefully you can help me. If not, I would be grateful if you could forward this email to the relevant person or let me know the appropriate person to contact.

I appreciate you taking the time to read my email and I look forward to hearing from you soon.

All the best,

Joe Bloggs
5th year Medical Student
Dudley Medical School

E-mail - joe.bloggs@dudleymedschool.ac.uk
Postal Mail - 33 Dudley Close, Dudley, DU D34, United Kingdom
Telephone - (+44) 7777 5757688

Awarding Body	Amount	Criteria	Closing Date	Contact Details
Edward Boyle Memorial Trust	6 x Up to £1000	Submit applications direct to the Dean of your medical school. Forms are available from your medical school registry from October.	31st January	W - http://www.rdinfo.org.uk/Queries/ListGrantDetails.asp?GrantID=2030 T - 020 7380 6700
The Medical Group/ Glaxo Wellcome Medical Fellowship	£400 for one student at each medical school + £1000 prize (b4 u leave)	Send elective proposal, CV, letter from hosting hospital and details of two referees.	31st March	E - gina.wheeler@medicinepublishing.co.uk T - 01235 555770
British Association in Forensic Medicine	£200 (on return)	For best forensic elective project. Winner asked to make presentation		W - www.sheffield.ac.uk/~bafm/stu.html E - p.d.lumb@sheffield.ac.uk T - 0114 273871
Medical Defence Union	£1,500, £1,000, £500 (b4 u go)	Answer questions and tie-breaker via website. Submit report and photographs on return.	31st August	W - www.the-mdu.com/studentm/elective/competition/index.asp T - 020 7202 1569
Pathological Society of Great Britain and Ireland	£75 per week (up to 12 weeks) (b4 u leave) + £100 for best report (on return)	For pathology placements. Must submit a report on return. Best report asked to make a presentation.	31st May	W - www.rcpath.org/index.php?PageID=144 administrator@pathsoc.org.uk T - 020 7976 1260

Awarding Body	Amount	Criteria	Closing Date	Contact Details
Royal Society of Tropical Medicine and Hygiene	2 x £500	Best account of work carried out during elective in a tropical or developing country. Candidates must be nominated by a member of staff from medical school who must provide a supporting statement.	31st December	W - www.rstmh.org/ English/index.html mail@rstmh.org T - 020 7580 2127
British Medical and Dental Student's Trust	Numerous. Up to £600			T - 0141 2215858
Royal Society of Medicine (Anaesthesia Section)	2 x £350 (b4 u leave)	For elective modules relating to anaesthesia.	2nd February	W - www.rsm.ac.uk/ students/studprizedetail. htm E - jo.parkinson@rsm.ac. uk T - 020 7902906
Royal Society of Medicine (Accident & Emergency Section)	£500	Emergency medicine related electives. Provide outline in less than 1000 words and CV. Make presentation on return.	31st March	W - www.rsm.ac.uk/ students/studprizedetail. htm E - jo.parkinson@rsm.ac. uk T - 020 7902906
British Society for Haematology	6 x Up to £600 (b4 u leave)	Asked to submit letter outlining elective and costs, along with confirmation from hosting institution and med school Dean. Must be haematology related.		

Awarding Body	Amount	Criteria	Closing Date	Contact Details
Renal Association of the UK	8 x £250 (b4 u leave)	Electives which include a significant renal element either clinical or research.		W - www.renal.org/ PrizesAwards/Prizes.html E- renal@immunology.org T - 020 8875 2413
Commonwealth Foundation	Up to 50 x £1000 (worldwide)	Two students are recommended by Deans of participating medical schools.		W - www. commonwealthfoundation. com/programmes/ programme.cfm?id=33
Royal College of Surgeons of England	4 x £500	For surgery electives in the developing world. Submit proposal, CV, confirmation from hosting institution and letter from med school.	3 May	W - www.rcseng.ac.uk/ surgical/research/awards/ preiskel_html E - research@rcseng.ac.uk T - 0207 869 6611
British Geriatrics Society for Health of the Aged	Up to £500 (b4 u leave)	Electives concerned with care of the elderly. Asked to submit report.		
Kabi Pharmacia Elective Grant	6 x £250	For electives in developing countries. Submit a proposal in 400 words.		
Child Health Research Appeal Trust	5 x £125 per week	Clinical attachments relating to child psychiatry or community health within the UK		
British Association of Plastic Surgeons	4 x £350 (b4 u leave)	For plastic surgery placements. Submit elective itinerary, costs and CV. Must submit a report on return.	31st January	

Awarding Body	Amount	Criteria	Closing Date	Contact Details
National Birthday Trust Fund (Wellbeing Charity)	2 x £250 (b4 u leave)	For electives in obstetrics or neonatal paediatrics. Submit CV and outline of your elective proposal.	11th June	W - www.wellbeing.org.uk/national.html E- bpeel.wellbeing@rcog.org.uk T - 020 7724 7725
British Nutrition Foundation/Nestlé Charitable Trust	12 x £500 (b4 u leave)	Electives concerned with nutritional problems encountered in a developing country. Send outline of proposal with reference from med school. Submit report on return.	31st January	W - www.nutrition.org.uk/awards/medical.htm E - postbox@nutrition.org.uk T - 020 7404 6504
Denis Burkitt Study Awards	10 x £750 (b4 u leave)	Students studying food and nutrition and their relationships to health and disease within any age group in developing nations. Send outline of proposal with reference from medical school. Submit report on return.	31st January	W - www.nutrition.org.uk/awards/burkitt.htm E - postbox@nutrition.org.uk T - 020 7404 6504
Royal College for General Practitioners And The Society for Academic Primary Care	£500 (b4 u leave)	Awarded for best proposal for elective project in General Practice/Primary Care. Submissions via your universities Dept of General Practice. Download application form. Winner to make presentation.	end March	W - www.rcgp.org.uk/rcgp/corporate/awards/rcgp_sapc_prize.asp E - mpatel@rcgp.org.uk T - 020 7851 3232

Still short of that all important total?? Here's some additional ideas for raising those few extra pounds.

Sell yourself - Many businesses have cash set aside to spend on good causes. Try smaller local firms first as they're often more willing to part with the cash. Offer them something in exchange – maybe you'd come in after you return and give a slide show. I managed to cover the cost of an entire month's desert expedition simply by offering to take photos of companies logos and products in the dunes – sure I felt daft holding up wet-wipes in front of a camel but it was worth it!!

Voluntary Service Overseas (VSO) - VSO is an organisation which will help support your travel and expenses if you get involved in one of their projects. They've many health attachments on offer from public education to local health development. Full details are available on their website.
www.vso.org.uk

Local Education Authority (LEA) - If you currently receive a maintenance grant you may be able to persuade your LEA to cough up some cash. Your elective is a compulsory part of the medical curriculum and as such you should get support towards travel and living expenses. As usual it depends where you live but it's definitely worth a try.

Take out a loan - If it's the only option left then it's worth considering. Paying back the cost of your elective when you're qualified and rolling in cash shouldn't be too much of a strain. It's better than looking back with eternal regret that you didn't spend your elective how you dreamed. Check out the 'professional study loans' offered by most high street banks.

before you leave ...

Visas - Have a good think about which countries you might want to visit before you leave the UK and organise the visas here – it's so much easier than negotiating when you arrive.

Bank Account - If you're staying for a long time in one country it can be worth opening a local bank account. It means you'll be able to withdraw cash for free. You can often open an account through one of their branches in the UK.

Some UK banks also allow you to withdraw cash overseas for free. For example, with *Barclays* you can withdraw dollars free from *Bank of America*, *Westpac Bank* in Australia and many others. It means you won't get charged expensive commission rates – or have to carry large amounts of travellers cheques with you!!

If you're going to an obscure destination make sure you check if there's actually a cash

machine before you leave. Try the VISA ATM checker -
www.visa.com/pd/atm/main.html

Vaccinations - Don't pay for travel vaccinations unless you have too. Most GP
practices still offer them for free. Move if necessary. Alternatively check with your
medical school GP co-ordinator. Avoid walk-in travel clinics, they'll charge you over
£100 for some vaccinations.

Get mobile - It's great to have a mobile phone when you're away ... though not so nice
when you get the bill on your return. Text messages are usually free to receive overseas
but calls can cost a fortune. A mobile phone can be invaluable for booking tickets,
meeting friends and giving your number to colleagues. Our advice is to buy a pre-pay
SIM card for one of the local networks. *The Carphone Warehouse* sell them for most
countries or you can get one from a local store when you arrive. For example, a
VirginMobile USA SIM card costs just $30.

Travel insurance - It's definitely worth getting good quality cover while you're away.
Most med students take out a policy with *BMA Services* which costs around £80 for the
duration of your trip. Unlike most other travel policies it offers emergency HIV
prophylaxis for needlestick injuries. Other cheap alternatives include *Insureandgo.com*
or *Studentinsure.co.uk*. Remember you won't be covered for ailments you have before
you leave so make sure you take enough inhalers, oinments and pills with you.
www.bmaservices.co.uk

Email - Sign-up for a good web-based email account. Add everyone to a single
mailing list so you can send them all an update quickly and easily with just one email –
especially if you're stuck in an expensive internet cafe.

Medical Indemnity - As long as you're a member of a medical indemnity insurer in
the UK, such as the *Medical Protection Society (MPS)*, you'll be covered against
mishaps overseas. It's worth getting a copy of the certificate before you leave.
www.mps.org.uk/student

Safe Travel - Have a quick glance at the foreign office website before you head to the
airport for the latest advice about the country you're visiting.
www.fco.gov.uk/travel

what am I allowed to do?

You'll often hear stories of medical students who claim to have perfected the art of
quadruple heart bypasses single-handed, or some other amazing procedure, whilst on
elective. When you probe a little further you'll find that their acts of surgical heroism
aren't quite what they seem. You should never agree to perform any procedure on
elective which you are not adequately supervised or feel competent to do.

Many doctors you'll meet will be unsure of your level of training and it's your responsibility to make sure you're safe. Remember all patients, no matter how poor the health system, have the right to respect, adequate consent and care.

On the other hand, you're likely to have the opportunity to experience some fantastic teaching whilst on elective. Make the most of it – you might even learn something!!

when you return

Getting back to the UK can be a real shock. Not only will you no longer get to spend lunch between the coconut palms on the beach, but you may even have to contend with exams. Returning can be a depressing affair and many people feel down for the first week or two.

On the positive side you'll be able to make all your mates jealous with your tan and stories of trauma in the tropics – now just pray that all those photos turned out ok!!

medical school **SURVIVAL GUIDE**

useful resources

The Budget Traveller's Guide to Sleeping in Airports
Unless you've run out of cash, or have a twelve hour wait for a flight it's best to avoid sleeping in airports, but if the worst happens this site tells you the comfiest places in most international airports to get some shut eye. It includes other places such as train and bus stations too. Who needs a hotel?!?
www.sleepinginairports.net

What's On
While you're bandaging in Brazil, or suturing in Stockholm you'll want to explore the local areas as well. This site lists events and festivals around the world. Whether it's flower shows in Florida or Salsa Parades in Sao Paulo you'll find the dates and information here.
www.festivals.com

Language Translation
Parlez vous francais?? One of the problems with organising an elective overseas is getting to grips with the language. Whether you're trying to communicate in French, Spanish, German or Chinese this handy tool allows you to instantly translate emails and websites for free here.
babelfish.altavista.com

Internet Café Guide
Just because you're stuck in the deepest darkest depths of Africa doesn't mean you have to lose touch with the rest of the world. Why not email all your mates back home and make them really jealous. This site lists the locations of over 2,000 internet cafes worldwide.
www.netcafeguide.com

Currency Checker
Finding converting your pounds to pesetas confusing? Are you getting ripped-off with your roubles? Well here's the answer. This site will work out how much your pounds are worth in virtually any other currency on earth. They'll even produce a handy conversion chart you can print and take with you!!
www.oanda.com

The World Fact Book
Did you know that the population of Algeria own 7.1 million radios?? Or that postage stamps are a major export of the Pitcairn Islands?? Find out everything you ever wanted to know about your destination in the World Fact Book produced by the CIA. It contains everything from literacy rates to HIV prevalence.
www.odci.gov/cia/publications/factbook

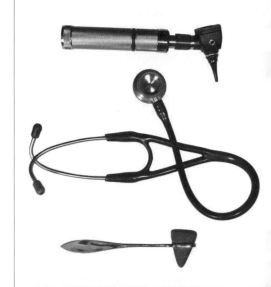

medical
school

SURVIVAL
GUIDE

careers

which path

When you told your school careers advisor that you wanted to be a doctor it all seemed pretty simple. You spend a few years at university, pass the exams, then go out and save the world. Unfortunately they didn't tell you there's a few more choices still to be made.

Now that you've made it to medical school the next step is deciding where you want to be in ten years time. Making the wrong decision can prove costly and the lack of advice we get from medical schools can literally send us 'career-ing' down the wrong path.

straight ahead

Looking at the timeline opposite your career path looks pretty simple. A few years at medical school, the endurance ride of the house officer years, pass a few exams and congratulations you're a consultant. Then it's off to the golf course and weekends in your seafront villa in the Cote D'Azur.

Sadly, life just isn't that simple. Despite your conviction that you want to be a brain surgeon, very few people end up in the specialty they first planned when they entered medical school. In fact, a high proportion of you won't follow this 'standard' career path at all.

With each rotation there's a chance you'll change your mind and decide that skin or psychiatry is more your thing. There's that fork in the road when you qualify between a surgical or medical career and there are problems trying to get into one of the more competitive specialties. And this is without taking into account all the other adult stuff, like the effect of relationships, kids and mortgages.

SURVIVAL
GUIDE | *medical school*

medical school
5-6 years
MBBS exam

Qualification

prho year
1 year

Registration

sho year
2-3 years
Membership exams

Membership

specialist registrar
5 years
Research or further degrees
Specialty training program

Certificate of Completion
of Specialist Training

consultant

And don't think your career only starts once you leave medical school. The path you'll end up taking is being mapped out right from the day you decide you wanted to be a doctor. The next five years play a crucial role in deciding whether you'll be a GP in Glasgow or a consultant dermatologist in Dudley. Here's some of the key decisions you'll have to make –

@ medical school

Medical school is the only time you'll have the chance to experience the different career options. You'll get rotated around all the main specialties, from psychiatry to genitourinary medicine. Once you've left medical school you won't have this option again so make sure you get the most from your experiences.

It should also be the time when you start to build that all important CV. Try to pick up a few relevant achievements along the way. Any projects, dissertations, conferences or audits relevant to your chosen specialty are invaluable when it comes to applying for jobs.

Remember, you may decide that you want to apply for one the specialised PRHO 'triple' rotations. You're going to have to show some interest and commitment if you want to fight off the competition.
(see the 'Applying for Jobs' section p121 for full information)

@ prho level

The PRHO year is your opportunity to experience the two worlds of medicine and surgery for real. After you qualify from medical school you'll have little over six months before you need to start thinking about applying for SHO posts.

You'll need to choose whether you want to apply for a two-year SHO rotation, or a single job for six months. There's advantages and disadvantages to both. The major consideration is whether you've decided which track to pursue. If you're not entirely sure if a career in surgery is for you, a six-month post (usually in A&E) will give you more time to decide.

Applying to a SHO post in the same hospital of your PRHO rotation will often give you the competitive advantage. You'll know a consultant who'll be able to put in a good word for you – providing you didn't kill too many patients.

Don't waste this year getting stressed about work and jobs though, it may be the only year between entering medical school until you reach consultant level that you've no exams to revise for. Make the most of your new found wealth and the little free time you've got.

Starting your SHO year is the beginning of the road to consultancy. You'll have decided by now whether you want to be dosing out pills on the wards, or be up to your elbows in body fat in the theatres. If you've decided on a career in General Practice you may have entered one of the training schemes.

But life doesn't get easier. In addition to coping with the long nights on call the nightmare of exams will start to take its toll just six months into the post. Your first membership exams can take place as early as February.

And if you thought that medical school exams were tough you haven't experienced anything yet. Pass rates for the Part I exams are often around 40 per cent – so don't get too upset if you don't make it first time round.

An audit (or two), a few presentations and a portfolio of publications should all be part of the plan during your SHO years. You'll also want to make a special effort to suck up to the consultant during your SHO post. A good reference counts for a lot.

Applying for a registrar post is a long-drawn and highly competitive affair, particularly for the more competitive specialties and teaching hospitals. There's a good chance you'll be hanging on as an SHO for quite a while before you get offered a post.

that little bit extra

Taking a year (or longer) to complete a Masters degree, or get stuck into some heavy research is a common choice either just before or during your registrar training. It's almost essential to pick up those popular consultancy posts.

This period is a bit like an elective just like you completed at med school. There's plenty of opportunities to go overseas or get involved in a subject that really interests you. Many even go on to obtain a PhD which certainly looks great on that CV.

@ registrar level

Registrar level is the penultimate stage before you reach that goal of consultancy. You'll still be working in the 'trenches' on the hospital wards but for the first time you'll have the responsibility to make life or death decisions. When things go wrong people will look to you for the answers.

Training as a specialist registrar takes at least five years, and there's a reason for this. In addition to passing the tough exams you'll need to know everything there is to know about your specialty and the wider field. Once you graduate to consultant level there's

medical school **SURVIVAL GUIDE**

no-one to call when things get scary at three o'clock in the morning.

Applying for a consultancy post isn't the same process as your previous jobs. With a consultant position it's more a case of being invited to take the post than fighting off the scrum of other applicants. More than ever it's going to be who you know and your reputation that counts.

@ consultant level

Twenty years after you first made that decision (or mistake) to become a doctor you've finally made it. You've now got the power, respect and fancy sports car that you always dreamed of.

But don't think that it's days out on the golf course for you now while you leave your team to run things in the hospital. The buck stops with you – no longer can you use the excuse "I'll just ask the consultant". People will take what you say seriously and at face value.

And don't think the career ladder ends here. There's medical directorships, positions on hundreds of committees and that all important private practice to keep you working hard.

As they say, medicine isn't a career it's a vocation. You never stop learning or reach the top. There's always new things, new procedures and new advances – and it doesn't look good if your SHO knows more than you do!!

SURVIVAL GUIDE *medical school*

careers outside medicine

So you've spent five years at medical school and gained the most desirable degree qualification anyone could wish for. You've proven your intelligence, ability to work as a team and determination to succeed. For you the opportunities are endless.

Whether you want to set-up your own business or work as a checkout assistant at *Tesco*, nobody can take that MBBS achievement away from you. The hard work is over.

Medical students often ignore the careers department at university. Sure, it's fine if your planning the usual trek up the ladder to consultancy, but if you fancy a life a little less ordinary then they'll be able to offer you all the advice you need.

Being seventeen is a little early to decide that you want to spend the rest of your life resecting portions of the small bowel. There'll be some of us who decide during the medical course that we'd rather not reach our fifties and still be spending our Monday mornings elbow deep in someone's abdomen.

Don't feel that just because you have a medical degree that it's the only option. There's a whole world of alternative careers out there. Here's a taster.

---

city careers

If you're craving to get your hands on some serious cash look out for the big city financial institutions who are desperate to recruit some newly qualified docs. With six years of tough studying under your belt, the Dr in front of your name and the knowledge of how to treat a financial trader whose just collapsed after losing £50 million on the bond market you're ideal for the city environment.

Not only will your take home salary be higher than your newly qualified colleagues but most city firms offer you a 'golden handshake' for signing up – this can be up to £10,000 in cash.

If you're interested in a career in capital bonds, stocks and securities have a chat with some of the institutions who have stands at careers fairs, or get in touch with the recruitment offices directly.

---

medical school   **SURVIVAL GUIDE**

science

If you prefer petri dishes to people there's plenty of opportunities in science – especially if you've had a few years of house officer training. Doctors are always required for research posts.

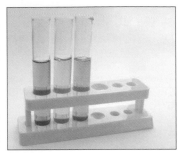

You could get involved in developing new treatments to cure deadly diseases, work as part of a team building micro-robots that clear sclerosed arteries, or aid a clinical trial testing the efficacy of existing medications. The possibilities are endless.

Have a look at the job opportunities in *New Scientist, BMJ Careers* or one of the online recruitment agencies.
www.newscientist.com

medical journalist

If people have always been commenting on your writing skills (and not just because of its poor legibility) then maybe you should 'pen' a career as a medical journalist. Your job would be to turn the complex, technical jargon that doctors use into the language that Mrs Brown of Macclesfield who has no GCSEs and thinks a spleen is a type of fresh water fish can understand.

Again, this is a field where that Dr in front of your name gives you an extra few steps up the careers ladder. Whether you'd prefer to write for the Sun, rabbit on about the MMR vaccine on Radio 4, or star on TV alongside Richard and Judy there's plenty of opportunities if you've got a little talent.

But be warned though, suddenly deciding to get your name in print isn't going to impress potential employers. Get some stories in 'trauma' or the 'studentBMJ' while at medical school. Feedback from the editors can be really useful to help you improve your writing. 'trauma' run yearly workshops for budding journalists every February. You can also join the Medical Journalists Association for just £10 per year which gives you access to both training and press events.
www.traumaroom.com
www.studentbmj.com
ww.mja-uk.org

management

Ten years ago the NHS used to be run by doctors – now it's the managers who are in charge. Running a hospital is just like running a factory, it's one big production line of patients who come in sick and go home better – well that's the theory anyway.

If you're well organised, motivated and enjoy a challenge (because the NHS is one BIG challenge) this may well be the career option for you. A undergraduate/postgraduate degree in hospital/public health management is almost essential and a good record of university committees and leadership roles will give you an advantage.

The team at NHS Careers will be happy to tell you more about management careers and how to apply.
www.nhscareers.com

So You Want to Be a Brain Surgeon?
This fantastic book covers all the main specialties ranking them by competitiveness, hours, pay and 'enjoyment'. There's also plenty of information about careers outside medicine.
Chris Ward, Simon Eccles
Oxford University Press, £15.95
ISBN - 0192630962

BMJ Careers
You're going to spend hours browsing the classified ads during the next two decades so there's no reason not to get acquainted now. This is where all those SHO, registrar, GP and consultancy posts get advertised. A fully searchable service is available free online along with useful careers articles
www.bmjcareers.com

Curriculum Vitae

*medical
school*

**SURVIVAL
GUIDE**

*applying
for jobs*

crack the cv

Despite your good looks and charm the first step to getting that perfect job is going to depend on how well you can sell yourself on paper. Creating a good CV is essential to improve your chances of ending up in the 'to interview' pile and not in the bin. You may not have achieved much at medical school but good CV technique can make you seem like a star candidate. Here's some advice.

sell yourself

The point of a CV is to sell yourself. Don't be modest. Your objective is to stand out from the other candidates and make sure they get discarded and not you. After writing each sentence of your CV ask yourself if it would make the consultant more likely to pick you. If not, discard it.

A sample CV is included on pages 124-127 including a cover letter. You can use this as a guide. Styles of CV vary so choose the one you're most comfortable with. Don't feel afraid to change the section headers if an alternative would suit your achievements better.

Stick to the main facts and avoid detail. The CV is used to screen those candidates who are worth calling for an interview. If the consultant wants to know more it's an extra incentive to put you through to the next stage. It will also give you something to talk about in the interview rather than just playing with your hair.

Get your parents, friends and housemates to check it. Spelling and grammar mistakes look really bad. Don't forget to check the cover letter too as this is often overlooked.

personalise your plea

Do your homework. If your consultant went to the same secondary school or has the same passion for toy trains make sure you mention it. After thirty years of medicine consultants like to talk about subjects other than your 4,000 word dissertation on gout occasionally, and that similar interest might just scoop you the job.

A useful tip is to do a search for the consultant in *Google* and the medical journals. You're likely to find his past publications, committees and his lap-time for the 100 metres sprint at his school sports day back in 1957.

tell the truth

Saying that you performed open-heart surgery in the depths of the Amazonian rainforest may sound impressive, but is likely to get you into trouble if you've never ventured further than Bradford. Stick to the truth. Trust and honestly is a vital quality for a doctor and one slip-up could cost you the job.

stand out from the rest

Handing your CV in on a few crumpled sheets of A4 is only going to speed your journey to the wastepaper basket. Remember you're applying for a job that's worth around £36,000. Investing a little time and cash will improve your chances.

Print your CV on a laser printer at college. Use quality 'laid' paper which you can pick up cheaply from *Rymans* or most stationers. If you want to knock the socks of the competition you could get it bound with a cover at *Kinkos* or other print store for a few pounds.

Remember it's all about making you stand out from the competition. To the consultant a well-presented, quality CV says a lot about the candidate and edges you up the interview list.

get referenced

You should normally include two references in your CV. In theory this should be one personal and one professional reference. For PRHO applications it's acceptable to use your personal tutor as one of your references and a member of the teaching staff as the other.

If you're applying as part of a matching scheme at your own university it's highly unlikely the reference will be consulted. For off-scheme jobs your 'professional' reference is likely to be asked to provide some sort of statement. For this reason make sure you have permission and that the person is likely to say a few good things about you.

JOE BLOGGS
33 DUDLEY CLOSE
DUDLEY
DU D34

TEL   0207 3620488
FAX   0870 1306985
JOE@TRAUMAROOM.COM

31ST MAY 2005

RE: SIX MONTH PRHO ROTATION - AUG 05

Dr T. Orture,

I would be grateful if you would consider my application for your 6-month PRHO rotation commencing August 2004. I have attached a copy of my CV.

Having spent time on your rotation I feel I have some perception of what this post would involve. I know the current house officers well and I am very enthusiastic to persue a career in this field.

If you have any further questions please feel free to contact me at the details above.

Thank you for taking the time to consider me for this post.

Yours faithfully,

Joe Bloggs

JOE BLOGGS, BA (HONS)

PERSONAL DETAILS

Address	33 Dudley Close
	Dudley
	DU D34

Tel	0207 3620488
Mobile	07777 123456

Email	joe.bloggs@dudleymedschool.ac.uk

Date of Birth	2nd May 1980		
Nationality	British	Sex	Male

QUALIFICATIONS

2000-01 University of Westminster, London
Intercalated Degree
BA (Hons) Medical Journalism

1991-98 Dudley Royal College, Dudley
A-Level Examinations
Geography A   Biology B   Chemistry C

CURRENT COURSES

1998-   Dudley Medical School
Expected qualification June 2005

Junior Medicine	MERIT
Junior Surgery	PASS
Junior OSCEs	PASS

Obstetrics and Gynaecology	MERIT
Psychiatry	PASS
Derm/A&E/Ortho/Rheum	PASS
GP/Care of Elderly	PASS
Neurology/ENT/Opth	MERIT
Paediatrics	PASS

Senior Surgery	PASS
Dermatology SSM	MERIT
Senior Medicine	MERIT

medical school **SURVIVAL GUIDE**

JOE BLOGGS, BSC

POSITIONS HELD

1999-present   **Dudley Surgical Society**
Executive Committee and Event Organiser.

1999-2000   **'trauma' Magazine**
News Editor for the UK edition.
www.traumaroom.com/uk

AWARDS

1999   **Dahle Prize for Obstetrics and Gynaecology**
National essay competition on Congential Deformities.

1999   **Young Science Writer of the Year Awards**
Highly Commended.

PUBLICATIONS

Feb 01   **Dudley Journal of Medicine**
Genetics – Should it be taught in medical school
or abolished forever?; DJM 2001; 328:345.
Co-author and survey researcher.

Aug 98   **'trauma' Magazine**
Feature on the Dudley Helicopter Emergency Service.

OTHER ACHIEVEMENTS

2002   **Dermatology Audit and Department Presentation**
Dudley University Hospital.

2000-2001   **'trauma'—Making a difference campaign**
Organising and raising sponsorship for cataract surgery
in Bangalore, India and equipment for a children's cancer
hospital in Sao Paulo, Brazil.

1999   **London Marathon in aid of Dudley Cancer Hospice**

1997   **Student Teaching Program**
Tutor for students lacking biology 'A'-level.

JOE BLOGGS, BSC

OTHERS

Qualified RYA sailing instructor

Dudley Men's Rowing Squad (2002-present)

REFEREES

Dr UR Sleepy
Department of Anesthesiology
Dudley University Hospital
Dudley
DU D45
Tel—0207 3620488

Dr IM Incharge
Dean of Student Affairs
Dudley Medical School
Dudley
DU D12
Tel—0207 3620488 ext. 3006

what is a matching scheme?

You may have heard of 'matching schemes' – the PRHO equivalent of a dating agency. It's a complicated system that few students, and even fewer medical school staff, understand. Here's some of the commonly asked questions.

What is a 'matching scheme'?
It's a complicated system used by medical schools for final year students to 'match' them with pre-registration house jobs. Most schools now use a computer program to match your preferences with the jobs available and consultant choices.

Why do I need to be in the 'matching scheme'?
You don't. There's no rule that says you have to find a job via your medical school matching scheme. Instead you can find a job off-scheme, or join the matching scheme of another deanery.

What are the benefits of a matching scheme?
It takes some of the stress out of finding a post. Most of the work to find a job will be done for you by the medical school or deanery.

What are the disadvantages?
You have no way of knowing if you are likely to get the job you wanted, and you could in theory end up with a job you really didn't want.

Do I have to take the job I'm allocated?
Yes, in most cases. When you apply to the majority of matching schemes you must agree to whichever you are allocated.

Will I get a job in the same trust?
Maybe. In London there are too many medical students for the number of jobs available. In other parts of the country it's the opposite. This is why many matching schemes have posts not just in their local hospitals but some further afield. As a result you may end up relatively far away.

Am I disadvantaged if I don't get a job in the field I wish to specialise in?
If you already have an idea of which specialty you wish to pursue no one will argue that a job in that field will be useful experience. However, if you don't get the job you had hoped for don't fear. The purpose of the first year is to introduce you to practical medical, having a good reference is much more important.

Things to check with the present house officers –

☐ Work load - how many hours? stress? on-call rotas? what the job entails?

☐ Facilities - canteen hours? accommodation? doctors mess? on-call rooms?

☐ Teaching - is it timetabled? consultant teaching? is there adequate support?

☐ Application - is there anything that would impress the consultant in your application? is the job competitive?

The consultant –

☐ Find out his/her special interests

☐ Job - what procedures and duties you will be expected to undertake?

☐ Teaching - when it happens? does he/she offer house officer teaching?

☐ Ask who assesses you? and who will write your reference?

Job hunting tips –

• The house officers and registrar may be asked their opinion of who gets the job by the consultant so suck up to them too.

• Check the current job banding which will give you an idea of the intensity of the job and number of antisocial hours.

• Ask to view the accommodation. This can vary dramatically between hospitals. Speak to the administrator, if you flirt enough you may be able to bag one of the better rooms.

• Search out students who have already been for interviews with the consultant and find out what they were asked and told.

the interview

Congratulations!! You've made it through the first stage of the selection process and have been called for an interview. Being grilled on your achievements by a bunch of strangers isn't the most pleasant of experiences, and even regular interviewees find it terrifying. Luckily a little preparation is all that's needed to keep the adrenaline rush down to a manageable level. Here's some advice.

rehearse your lines

There's a limited number of questions that you can be asked during an interview. Spend time thinking which are the most likely and what your best response would be before the day. Once you've got your perfected answers rehearse them over and over.

Always think about how your answer comes across to the interviewer. Remember that they're looking for someone with enthusiasm, is reliable, efficient and doesn't make mistakes. Persuade them of this and the job is yours.

There's a few questions that come up again and again. They're tough and designed to trip you up. Work out your response in advance. We've included a few examples below. Don't repeat them verbatim, instead adjust them to suit you.

"Why did you apply for this job?"

Options -

- I know your current house officers, Julie and Simon. They've always mentioned great things about the firm and your team.
  (You should have already spoken to both the PRHOs and SHOs)

- My vascular surgery rotation in fourth year was probably the most enjoyable and interesting firm at medical school. It would be great to work in a similar field and this is definitely a specialty I would consider as a future career. Your rotation was recommended to me as one of the best in the trust.

SURVIVAL GUIDE | *medical school*

"Why should I pick you instead of the other candidates?"

Options -

* I realise that this is a very competitive rotation and I'm sure a lot of other good candidates have applied. I can only mention again my enthusiasm for this field and to medicine as a whole. I'm not one of those people who disappear as soon as all the jobs are done as I really like to get involved in all aspects of the firm.

* Based on what I've heard from your current house officers I feel I would integrate really well into your team and my past experience of this hospital should make the transition a lot easier.

* [If you've got any relevant experience or achievements to this rotation make sure you mention them.]

"What's your worst quality?"

Options -

* I'm a bit of a perfectionist, which I guess is good in a career such a medicine where you can't afford to make mistakes, but it sometimes slows me down a little. I'm doing my best to overcome this.

* I honestly find medicine fascinating and over the last five years of medical school I seemed to have taken a greater interest in it than most people. It's made passing the MBBS course that bit easier but I feel also that I've sacrificed my life outside medicine a little.

"Do you have any questions?"

Options -

* No. I had a few, but your team answered them for me when I spoke to them before applying for this position.
* I am very keen on pursuing a career in surgery. Will there be any opportunities as a PRHO to be present in theatre?

Another good idea is to hold mock interviews with your mates. You can swap good lines and pick out irritating habits before it's too late. Videoing your performance is a great way to see how you come across to the interviewers.

medical school   **SURVIVAL GUIDE**

on the day

Leave yourself plenty of time to get there, and allow an extra fifteen minutes to catch your breath, find a glass of water and straighten your tie in the hospital toilets. Don't forget to switch your mobile off before you enter and don't arrive with headphones sticking out of your ears.

Be polite to the secretary as they often give their opinion on who they liked – whether the consultant asks for it or not. Smile and thank everyone for taking the time to see you.

during the interview

Throughout your interview remember that you want them to employ you. Be professional and confident. It's important that you come across as a 'nice' person, even if you're not, as the consultant is going to have to spend a lot of time with you.

Sit smartly. Don't fidget or bite your nails, try clasping your hands together if you feel you're going to struggle with this. Smile, but don't intimidate the interviewers.

Feed their egos. Consultants like to be loved and respected. Any compliments you can throw their way, without going overboard, can help get you extra points. Telling them that their firm has a great reputation among students and house officers is a good one.

after the event

Don't spend too much time reflecting on how things went, but do pick out the answers you gave well and those you need to work on before the next interview. Treat each one as a practice for the next and you'll gradually improve.

If you don't get the job don't feel embarrassed about asking why. Feedback is extremely useful and it will help to identify where your weaknesses are, and what you need to work on. Most consultants are happy to do this if you approach them via their secretary.

JustGraduates
Specifically aimed at students and recent graduates it has advice on how to find weaknesses in your CV and correct them. The interview advice section covers topics like 'Answering Awkward Questions' and 'Researching'. Check it out.
www.justgraduates.net/JustCareers/careeradvice.asp

Medical Job Interview: Secrets for Success
A good book for perfecting your CV and last minute advice for that all important medical interview. It focuses on clinical jobs but has useful advice for the PRHO application process too.
Colin Mumford
Blackwell Science, £9.99
ISBN - 0632055278

BMJ Careers
Packed with loads of articles on all aspects of job hunting from finding the right job for you, advice with the CV and how to approach the interview process you'll find it all here.
www.bmjcareers.com

medical
school

**SURVIVAL
GUIDE**

*being a
real doctor*

working out

Soon you'll find yourself with an MBBS after your name and a Dr in front. Six-years will have flown by and it's now time for you to make your first real appearance on the wards. You've had questions right through medical school that you wanted answers too, so here's the PRHO work-up.

pre-registraion house what?

Just because you're 'qualified' doesn't mean you're a 'registered' doctor. There's limits to what you can do and requirements that you must complete. Here's your questions answered courtesy of the General Medical Council –

So what's the purpose of the pre-registration year before I become a 'proper' doctor?
The pre-registration year is the final year of basic medical education. It has two purposes:
(1) to enable pre-registration house officers (PRHOs) to put into practice the key skills that they have learned and apply knowledge gained during undergraduate medical education
(2) to enable PRHOs to demonstrate that on completing general clinical training, they are ready to accept with confidence the duties and responsibilities of a fully registered doctor and to begin training for specialist medical practice.

How long does my PRHO year have to be?
At present, the twelve months of full time training must include at least three months in medicine and three months in surgery, and may include up to four months in general practice. The whole of the training must be completed satisfactorily.

What are the benefits and responsibilities?
Provisional registration with the GMC gives PRHOs the rights and privileges of a doctor. In return PRHOs must meet the standards of competence, care and conduct set by the GMC, as outlined in its booklet *Good Medical Practice*. PRHOs must also accept responsibility for their own learning.

Can I do locum work while a PRHO?
PRHOs are in the process of completing their basic medical education and must not be allowed to undertake locum appointments.

Will I get regular teaching?
PRHOs should have a weekly programme of educational seminars/group discussion covering topics of interest and value to them.

Will I have help when I need it?
PRHOs must have available to them in the hospital, at all times of the day or night, a more senior member of staff in an appropriate specialty who can provide cover and help. The arrangements for providing cover must be explicit and known to both the PRHO and the senior doctor. In the interests of both the PRHOs and their patients, house officers must never be in the position where their only source of help is outside the hospital.

I heard stories about PRHO's doing menial jobs like chasing up results without proper teaching?
PRHOs are often expected to undertake tasks that do not require medical skill. These include
- repeated intravenous injections through established infusion line
- portering
- finding beds for admissions
- chasing up and obtaining x-rays and the results of other routine investigations
- filing and other strictly clerical work
- explaining the cancellation of admissions

These tasks are of no educational value and PRHOs should not be expected to perform them unless the circumstances are exceptional.

Do I meet the previous house officers before I start?
There should be a formal handover with the outgoing PRHO. On or before the date of taking up your post, you should be given a contract of employment. You should also be given a learning agreement at your first meeting with your educational supervisor.

Is there a requirement to live in hospital accommodation?
PRHOs must be resident in the hospital or health centre where they are working, or 'conveniently near to it'.

Who is in charge of my education?
Educational supervisors are appointed to look after the educational needs and general welfare of PRHOs, and their principal task is to make sure that you achieve the goals and objectives of general clinical training, as specified by the GMC. They are also responsible for signing the Certificate of Satisfactory Service when you complete each post.

Is registration automatic after the PRHO year?
Most PRHOs complete their general clinical training in twelve months and proceed to full registration thereafter, but a small minority do not. Some PRHOs, for example, may require a further period of training at that grade. Your educational supervisor is expected to assess your clinical and educational progress carefully, and you should not assume that a certificate will always be forthcoming.

Will I be asked to perform difficult procedures?
You should not be asked to undertake a clinical task for which you have not been adequately prepared. If at any time you are in doubt, you should ask for help from more experienced colleagues. No senior doctor will criticise you for this.

clinical skills you'll need

Here's the sort of skills you'll be expected to have when you hit the wards with your shiny new doctor's badge –

a. Obtain valid consent
b. Calculate drug dosage accurately
c. Write a prescription
d. Procedures involving veins*
   - venepuncture
   - insert cannula into peripheral vein
   - give intravenous injections
   - mix and inject drugs into intravenous bag
   - use a pump to give drug treatment
e. Give intramuscular and subcutaneous injections*
f. Arterial blood sampling
g. Suturing
h. Perform an ECG*
   - conduct an exercise ECG
i. Basic cardiopulmonary resuscitation
j. Perform basic respiratory function tests*
k. Administer oxygen therapy safely
l. Correct use of a nebuliser
m. Gastrointestinal
   - insert nasogastric tube*
   - proctoscopy
n. Bladder catheterisation
o. Lumbar puncture (for diagnostic purposes)
p. Control of haemorrhage

* = should not be routinely carried out by PRHOs

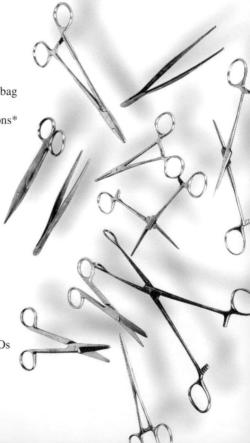

It can be pretty daunting on your first day as a house officer. We asked our PRHO correspondent down in the trenches, *Paul Vig*, for some advice –

stay cool

Be calm. People will always cut you some slack during your first year. They were all house officers too. Just remember –

THE GOLDEN RULE – IF YOU DON'T KNOW, ASK!!

get booked

Remember no-one knows everything, not even your consultant!! This is essential for the benefit of the patient – never mind your pride, leave that at the hospital entrance. You are on a very steep learning curve, and will have a few knocks on the way up. The *Hands on Guide for House Officers* and *Oxford Clinical Handbook* will provide many answers and both are essential for those first weeks.

forget the fabricating

Another important rule is don't assume. This means that you have to find out the facts for yourself, especially when you are questioned. Start fabricating and you'll start digging your own pit to fall into. No-one is perfect, so own up.

make friends

Get to know the ward staff, your team and the layout of the hospital. It makes the day more pleasant if you actually get to know the people you work with, and where to find the blood gas machine in the small hours.

get ur stats sorted

Essentially you are the first line in the pyramidal medical system. You set the ball rolling, your SHO and SpR give it impetus and the consultant fine tunes the motion. Basic tests and examinations are the key. When seeing an acutely ill patient get everything ready before getting in touch with seniors, otherwise you will look stupid when they ask for the JVP. Always get your stats sorted first!!

be social with the sho

Your SHO is your primary lifeline, become friends and work will be so much better. If possible have your lunch break with them to discuss clinical (and social) matters. Lunch is essential – remember we are human too!!

nurture the nurses

Always tell nursing staff of management changes that your team make. Ideally get a nurse to go round with you and your SHO. If you see a patient and change their

treatment regime and just write in the notes, you may
as well have done nothing. Communication is the key.
To quote from a wise old SHO – "you can survive
if you don't get on with your consultant, but if
you don't get on with the nurses you've had it!!"
So be nice. A smile costs nothing.

patient power

An ideal to aspire to – work for your
patients not for your consultant. For ward
rounds get all test results in order and
you'll look professional. Try to get to
know the patients if possible, and that
Barthel index if working on the geriatric
side – bed-blocking is a major issue and the earlier
social services know the better.

hide and seek

Find all the patients. It may seem a strange task but
otherwise you'll look very stupid during consultant ward
rounds, especially handbacks to your team from other on-
calls. A quick 'ward sweep' by going round all the main
wards can be a life saver especially after a harrowing day on call. Make a patient list,
preferably on computer, and update it daily if you can with the ward, date of birth,
hospital number and working diagnosis – legally you should password protect all
documents on computer. Some trusts are ano-retentive about this!!

in summary

Discharge summaries, often called TTO's (medicines 'to take out'), are important.
Some of your colleagues do them to the entry standard for the Booker prize but just
include the basics. Try to imagine if you were the GP would this scrawled note mean
anything to you? To keep the nursing staff happy do the TTO the day before discharge,
or if in a huge rush write the pills section and come back to do the medical summary
before it gets faxed to the GP.

accidents in emergencies

On-call admitting in accident and emergency can be the best part of the job but can
also be a nightmare if your team solely deal with the admitting day. Here you'll have to
cover your regular patients and then admit more!! On the positive side you get to test
your ability to diagnose and manage acutely ill patients. You will be surprised how
long it takes to clerk a patient initially but it does get faster when you get slicker with
that steth and tendon hammer.

on-call cover chaos

On-call ward cover is a nightmare. One way to reduce this is to deal with your own workload and don't run off at five (this may mean staying till 8pm!!). If one of your colleagues always skives off then have words with him or her as a group. Sort out changes to an evil rota early if you want time off or need to swap a day or weekend. Be flexible and others will too. Book leave early – some devious people do it on the first day!!

don't get furious with the forms

Accident forms are a pain, especially when covering geriatric patients who can make a habit of jumping over cot sides. They are an official trust document, but try and write in the notes as well so the team next day know. GCS, general obs, pupils and acuity, skeletal survey mainly suffice. But remember – do examine the patient properly as *you* sign on that dotted line.

breaking bad news

Breaking bad news is difficult – leave this to seniors but eventually you will have to do it yourself. Try and get to sit in with an experienced doctor to see how it's done. It's also useful to take a 'back-up' along in the form of a senior staff nurse. Seat everyone in a side room, take tissues and leave your bleep elsewhere.

help me—stat!!

Crash calls are generally not successful unless the patient is on CCU following an MI. Don't be put off by this and just follow the procedure – main tasks for PRHOs will be getting venous access or taking blood samples for immediate analysis. It's quite exciting at the beginning, but in the early hours when you can tell they've been gone for a while you soon realise it really isn't!!

'ash cash'

Cremation forms are lucrative at £50 a go. It involves a trip to the morgue to see the body, assess that there is no pacemaker and to check that no radioactive implant has been fitted. 'Ash cash' is therefore pretty easy. Death certificates are a tad harder to get to grips with. Remember it has to be sequential and things must follow on. You'll often be surprised to have a debate with your team about what actually did it!! Have a chat to the coroner too – they are often quite nice.

surgical stresses

In surgical jobs your team are often few and far between. Trips down to theatre may be needed if bleeps aren't answered and the patient issues are urgent. Also, there are the nightmarishly early starts compared to medicine. All the patients seem to be on iv fluids so put out daily blood test forms for the hugely underrated phlebotomy service, and sort out post-op pain control. Remember that pain really does hurt!!

pre-admit anxiety

Running a pre-admission clinic for elective ops can be fun – you almost feel like a real doctor!! Anaesthetic risk must be assessed. And do they really still need surgery for those haemorrhoids?? Explain the risks and benefits of each op but you legally cannot consent unless you can do the operation yourself. Instead you can sort out pre-op therapies ie. bowel preps, write up a drug chart and the make sure the clerking is legible. Occasionally show your face in theatre and try to get to know the anaesthetist there too.

reward yourself

Remember that you get paid for this fun!! Even though occasionally you can do 90+ hours you still get to take home well over £450 a week, with no rent. Time for that DVD player, widescreen tele, dinner at the Ivy, new GTI and private tour of Seychelles, Learjet. So enjoy it. Let the bank know so they stay off your back regarding the overdraft, and get your credit cards changed too – both to impress your non-medic friends and that girl at the petrol station!!!

Your PRHO year soon flies by and then you make that quantum leap to SHO level. You may even get your own House Officer to look after and nurture (and be responsible for their mistakes!!).

Paul was a PRHO at St. Thomas's Hospital, London.

useful resources

The Hands-on Guide for House Officers

Everything you could want to know and more. As well as clinical information on how to complete charts and perform minor procedures there's tips on how to stay organised and deal with hospital contracts. Essential for those first few weeks.
Blackwell Science, £16.50
ISBN - 0632053313

BMA PRHO Booklet

The BMA have been fighting to improve accommodation, working conditions and training for PRHOs for years. This booklet contains all the information on what you are entitled to as a junior doctor and what to do when things go wrong. It's free for BMA members.
www.bma.org.uk
Tel - 020 7387 4499

GMC - Initial training as a new doctor

The definitive guide to what you should and shouldn't be doing as a PRHO. You can also read the requirements to enable full registration.
www.gmc-uk.org/med_ed/default.htm

medical school   **SURVIVAL GUIDE**

medical
school

SURVIVAL
GUIDE

the team

In addition to those who submitted ideas and suggestions for this book the following people and organisations deserve thanks for their input –

Richard Partridge, Muhunthan Thillai, Kirk Smith, Dargan Miller, Sabina Dosani, Laura Caley, Ellen Welch, the GMC, David Armstrong, Shiva Dindyal, Deboshree Basu-Choudhuri, Marianna Thomas, the BMA, Sanj Gupta, Sarah-Jane Walton, Minha Rajput, Rameen Shakur, Deborra Radcliffe, London Deanery, Anna McDonald, Sheraz Younas, Nicholas Hamilton, Bruno Rushforth, Bilal Jamal, Mary Crouch, Wendy Brown, Sai Duraisingham, Sarah Spencer, Catriona Munro, Sarah Maidment, Paul Vig, Katerina Denediou.

medical
school

SURVIVAL
GUIDE

index